ALL THIS HAPPENED, MORE OR LESS

Jayne A. Quan

Skein Press
2022

First published by Skein Press in 2022
www.skeinpress.com

A CIP catalogue for this title is available from the British Library.
ISBN 978-1-915017-01-7

A version of the essay 'Better, sweeter' was previously published in
Banshee, issue 10.

Cover design and layout: Éilís Murphy of Folded Leaf
Cover image: original photograph by Karolina Grabowska
Printed by Walsh Colour Print, Co. Kerry, Ireland
Skein Press gratefully acknowledges the financial support it receives
from the Arts Council.

For Emily and Kaedyn
who finally, forever,
and only
meet on this page.

Author's note

I used the opening line of Kurt Vonnegut's *Slaughterhouse-Five* as the title for this book: *All this happened, more or less.*

In transformation, transition, grief and growth there is always more and less. These essays are an ode to all that loss and gain, literally, metaphorically, in all the ways that matter. From my brother to my chest to love to weight to muscle, from Ireland to Los Angeles, from depression to elation – all this happened, more or less.

I wrote these essays when I was a particular person at a particular point in time. They centre my experience with a medically assisted transition as a person who identifies as both transmasculine and non-binary – an experience that I chose and that I was privileged to access. But I am one person, one trans person, one non-binary person. I am a single thread in the rich tapestry of human experience, and these words woven together here should never be taken as the paradigm of all trans, non-binary and queer experiences.

Everything in these pages happened as I remembered. All is as accurate as my memory allows. This is how I remember things happening and this is how I have written them down.

Why have I written things down? I wrote to try to make sense of it all. The first year after my brother died was chaos, highs and lows interrupting one another at every turn. Writing things down was a way for me to space out the major events and try to make a timeline so that I could give each piece of my life the attention it deserved. From his cremation to my top surgery to getting accepted into school to falling in love to arriving in Ireland – I hadn't reflected; I had simply come and gone.

These essays, these meditations on certain intersections of my life, are not the archetype for transness or queerness, nor are they the ideal examination of grief. These pages are a way to anchor and ground myself in my experiences because I wasn't sure I truly experienced them.

Vonnegut ended his book with *Poo-tee-weet?*

But this ends with a final flip of the page.

CONTENTS

Both sides now

People do not die for us immediately, but remain
bathed in a sort of aura of
life which bears no relation to true immortality but
through which they
continue to occupy our thoughts in the same way as
when they were alive. It
is as though they were traveling abroad.

— Marcel Proust

Baby A

There are things that I remember very well and things that I have forgotten completely.

I remember standing at the incubator of my smallest brother, staring at his purple skin, the smallness of him, the bigness of the hole he would leave, thinking, *I will remember this forever.*

And I do. I will.

I wonder how many times I have stood on the precipice of my life changing, thinking, *I will remember this forever*, and then, as humans do, forgot. How many things have I left in the past?

How many things have I detached and unknown from myself?

Let me start at the beginning.

—

I was told that I was born with a purplish hue to my skin, with my umbilical cord wound tightly around my neck. My parents were twenty and twenty-one years old and I was there when they got married in a chapel in Reno, Nevada. Not yet alive, but present nonetheless.

I've seen only one photo of my parents' wedding. My mother is wearing ugly lace and a typical eighties perm and my father has terrible facial hair. I know I'm there in that photo because I work backwards from the date on the photo with all the perverse curiosity of an adolescent who finds a picture of their young parents' wedding. I am there: an accident, but wanted, in the end (or at the beginning).

If I think what happened did happen, then I must be seventeen weeks and two days into gestation. A fleshy mass the size of a pomegranate just deciding to turn cartilage into bone. An idea with lungs.

My brothers were born a more severe shade of purple at twenty-two weeks and five days gestation.

I was sixteen years old when they were born into this world and I was seventeen when one passed away.

But I'm getting ahead of myself.

—

When my sister was born, I was told that I looked at her with a tight smile. I was three years old. In the first known photo of us together, I am smiling with my lips pursed. It looks more like a grimace. My sister's round head is pink, wrinkled and a bit bloated in the way that newborn babies' heads are, and her eyes are closed. She is new to the world in that photo. New to breathing and screaming and crying. New to people and places and things. New to life.

My mother insists that I asked when we could take my sister back to wherever she came from.

She also insists that I asked for a brother.

I would end up with four . . .

. . . and then three . . .

. . . and then . . .

These memories are told to me over and over again until they become believable, until I swear I can remember them myself. Anecdotes like this – being told who I am before I knew what kind of person I could be – are transplant memories. Memories I just accept as my own.

'Don't you remember . . . ?'

'Yes,' I say. But I don't and I wonder if I should.

The yellow light of the hospital room, the bed sheets, the linoleum floors – I think I know these details, but perhaps I've made them up, filling in the colours and textures like painting by numbers. By not remembering, did I forget something important? Was that a memory I should have kept forever? Sometimes I think that I can remember the grime of a window that overlooked a hospital parking lot, but that can't be right. I don't think I was tall enough to see out of the window.

I wonder if I stood at the rail of my mother's hospital bed, looking down at my newborn sister, the delicate pink freshness of her, and thought, *I will remember this forever*. And maybe I did, because forever to a three-year-old was probably a week. But it's more likely that my concept of remembering and my concept of forever had yet to form, and for me, the day my sister was born was just a day.

I asked my mother about that day and she says that she

remembers the drive to the hospital in the morning and the ease with which my sister was born (in heavily implied contrast to my birth). She said she remembers my father going across the street so that he could eat a slice of pizza while she laboured. It was a burrito when I was born. She said she remembers my aunt bringing me over in the afternoon. She said she remembers that it was a bright and clear day.

I must take her word for it.

—

This is how my memory works.

I am standing in a big house in Atherton. There are two dogs. There are three dogs. There is one dog. There are people here who I am related to because my stepmother is related to them and I think that I am polite and that I smile correctly and that I shake hands with a man named Uncle Sam who has triplets (all of whom will be smarter than me, I am later told, in another memory). This is how I meet my brother. I am fifteen.

I am eight. My parents are angry and fighting and getting a divorce. My father flings a box of my mother's belongings into the cul-de-sac after an angry conversation. She must call again, and I must pick up, because I crouch in the street with our cordless phone pressed against my ear and I cannot remember what she's said to me now, but I am picking things up off the newly redone asphalt. A delicate chain with interlocking gold links and papers. The asphalt is black and coarse and slightly damp from yesterday's rain. It smells like moist garden pebbles.

I am nineteen and I'm drunk on a street called Sabado Tarde, making out with a boy whose face I will never remember; but I remember that I let him kiss me because I would like to be kissing the girl his friend is kissing. He's pressed me up against a black car. The streetlamp above us paints everything a terrible orange.

I am nine and my aunt is pushing three books – slightly too big – into my hands, telling me that I will like them very much. They are the first three books in the Harry Potter series.

I am twenty-three and I've just come out of a movie with a friend at the Pavilion Theater on the northwest corner of Bartel-Pritchard Square. I cannot remember what movie we saw but it's the first snowfall of the season in Brooklyn, New York, as we step out into the cold air. We are both instantly ecstatic, the two of us who were born and raised in the sunshine of California. We run up Prospect Park West laughing as the snow sticks to the ground. I draw a gigantic penis onto the hood of a Toyota Prius parked on the corner of 13th Street.

I am twenty-eight. I slide into the sun-warmed seat of a 2008 Sebring. I can smell my barista shift wafting off me – stale espresso and dried dairy and that smell that is always associated with food service. The girl I've been sleeping with for two weeks is smiling at me even though I have settled into the passenger's seat with a sigh that deflates my body. I'm so tired I feel like I'm barely holding myself together. I see her hand move like she wants to run it across my cheek and I see her eyes flicker to my mouth. I ask her for a kiss even though we are not yet official. Even though I want to be. Even though we will be.

–

I am sixteen. It's spring break, my sophomore year of high school. My dad and my stepmom have just started telling people that they are pregnant. With twins. I am delighted at the prospect.

It's the spring break when people start asking me if I know what I want to study in college, where I might start applying. For me, these are loaded questions. Last summer my girlfriend broke up with me even though she still invites me to her empty house so we can have sex while her mother works and her father is away on one of his many business trips. We're thinking of going to college together.

I go to high school in Southern California – 426.6 miles away from where my father and stepmother live in San Francisco, so I spend every academic break swapping friends for family, which makes me an angry, angsty teenager on the verge of change.

My father wakes me up sometime on the morning of 9 April. I think he sounded calm, but even now I'm not sure. What does my father sound like when he is nervous? Have I ever heard him panic?

'We have to go to the hospital,' he says.

I don't remember looking at him. I don't remember his face as he says these words to me.

'I'll have my phone. Watch the kids.'

He leaves and I go back to sleep. Or at least I must have, because the next memory I have is daylight streaming through the windows with no notification on my cell phone that my parents have tried to reach us.

My grandfather picks us up from the house. Or maybe it's my grandmother. Someone takes us into the city where the hospital is, where something has happened. One of the hospital corridors is wide and sand-coloured. Everything from the wall to the carpet to the linoleum floor is light brown and earthy. Someone who knew my mother from high school is here and says I look just like her. Or maybe that memory happened during a different visit to the hospital.

We are quiet, the four of us children. We are well-behaved and pleasant to be around. Nobody tells us anything except that something bad has happened. My memory skips along scenes like a stone across a lake. People in a room. My grandfather's annoying girlfriend. My stepmother's brother who doesn't talk to us anymore. His wife who is the reason he doesn't talk to us anymore. The sheets stacked in a cupboard I wasn't supposed to open. My stepmother in the hospital bed with that downcast look on her face, a look that I know now is fear and grief, but back then was incomprehensible. The sterile, almost acrid smell of disinfectant. I can't remember a single doctor.

And then, suddenly, standing at the neonatal incubator.

The room is warm and dimly lit. It's quiet in the way that libraries are quiet, as if there is another world you've stolen away from just outside the door. Tungsten lamps are somewhere in the room, throwing yellow and marigold across every reflective surface. There's a lump in my throat and I'm holding back tears because this is not the way that life is supposed to be brought into the world. But it is. It was.

They didn't have names at first.

That's another scene from my disjointed memories of our time in the hospital. I'm sitting in a bookstore across the street, flipping through baby names. We had certain criteria. Baby A and Baby B needed names that started with the letter *k* and also had a *y*. These were realistic goals for us at sixteen, thirteen and ten years old. Our two-year-old brother was too small to come with us, so it was just us three flipping through book after book, trying to kill time. I watched people walk into and out of the hospital through a grimy window in the bookstore.

But as I stood at the incubator, they did not yet have their names.

Baby A is 1 lb 4 oz. Baby B is 1 lb 5 oz. At twenty-two weeks, they were supposed to be almost the size of eggplants. Because they are twins, they are not quite that size, but they match the hue – violet with tones of yellow; the emergency C-section meant they had to be removed from the birth canal. Unready to be born; things bruise easily when plucked before their time.

In that quiet room where too-small babies are kept to prolong their existence, I stare at the purple skin of my Baby A brother. I stare at the smallness of him, how he can fit into my hand. I imagine the size of the hole that he would leave inside of me if he were to go.

I think I will remember this forever.

And I do. I will.

—

Baby A passed away on 23 April 2007. He was two weeks old.

This is how my memory of him works: I loved him wholly and I am, to this day, devastated by his loss. I know more about every person I've had a passing conversation with than I do about my youngest brother. And yet I know that I loved him.

The hole his death left in me was immense and only seemed to grow as time went on. When large stars die, they explode into supernovas, expanding from their centres in light and colour. When large-enough stars die, those supernovas collapse and form a singularity – a point where nothing can escape: a black hole.

Let me tell you how a black hole is formed inside of a person. Let me show you.

Let me start at the end.

Baby B

In 1998, my great-grandmother died of a stroke. I think she was found in her bathroom, on the floor, after nobody had heard from her for a day. It was the first time I'd seen my father cry. My parents were already separated by then, and when my mother came to take me to school, she asked, 'What happened?'

'Something happened to Grandma,' I think I said. Maybe I did. Maybe I didn't.

But I remember my father sitting at the table in the dining room with his head in his palm, bent forward like he was about to fall, like he wanted to dive into the ground headfirst.

My father says my great-grandmother did not look like herself when she was in her casket. He made them close it because she was bloated and disfigured. The photo by the head of the coffin was how I remembered her before death had transformed her on the cool bathroom tiles, before the formaldehyde tried to keep the rot at bay, before they tried to paint her sunken grey skin with a small blossom of blush.

Before my father bent at the waist, caught between falling and sitting.

—

My mother's side is Catholic.

I have seen everyone who has died on that side in the aftermath of their demise.

I can't remember what year it was when we had to sit with Tito, my great-uncle, in the living room, saying our prayers over and over and over again. I am not Catholic. I don't even believe in God, though I think she must be beautiful.

Our Father who art in Heaven. Hallowed be thy name. The Lord's Prayer. Thy Kingdom come. Thy will be done. On Earth as it is in Heaven. There's a lot of that. A lot of repeating and reciting in a dark room while he lies right there on an elevated platform. How old was I that I thought it so funny that he was dead in the living room? I think he would have thought that was funny, too. He was the darkest relative I had. Tito was brown – dark brown like the bark of a tree. He was kind and silent like one, too. And when he was in his casket, dead in the living room, that brown skin was taut against his cheeks, and the bones in his hands seemed to stretch the skin over his knuckles. Still silent. Still kind.

Give us this day our daily bread.

I had never seen him wear a suit before. The white shirt against his dull skin seemed strange. Like a bed dressed with the wrong kinds of sheets. A table with mismatched placemats. Something wrong.

And forgive our trespasses as we forgive those who trespass against *us*.

—

Baby B was ten years old when he passed away, three days after my sister's twenty-fifth birthday.

His legs were skinny and his knees were knobby. He was a boy who sat like an old man and when he spoke to you, it seemed important that you listened. He was giving you the gift of wisdom. And when he spoke, he sounded like Donald Duck; his vocal chords had frozen because of his significantly premature birth. I was the oldest of five and he was my favourite. Now I am the oldest of four and I love them all equally.

We flew last-minute from California to Texas when he got sick from an infection. He'd been in Texas for six months, placed on a transplant list for a new lung. Because of that infection, he would never get a new lung. Sometimes I imagine he's still on that transplant list.

But he was not conscious when we got there. He would not be conscious again.

He would never again say that he hated the colour I had dyed my hair or point at my sister's nose ring and ask 'What's that?' or rub at my tattoos and tell me that he didn't like that they were there forever. He would never again.

I'm not sure if a dead body usually turns yellow that quickly. I think it might have been the medications. Regardless, his pale body turned yellow. My family wailed. I wailed. I had never been so hurt in my life.

If you're wondering how he died, the answer is simple: his mother, a registered nurse, removed his breathing tube and he went. Where? I don't know. Nobody has been able to come back and answer that question for us. But he went. Parts of us did too.

And lead us not into temptation.

The body grows cold surprisingly fast. We removed the plethora of tubes that connected him to monitors and machines that were supposed to be lifesaving, but ended up being only life-prolonging. The people at Texas Children's Hospital must have been overwhelmed by the swell of our grieving family – adult children with their parents and grandparents. They stepped to the side while we cleaned our little boy. A nurse did remove his IV, though. That I remember. When she did, she held a piece of gauze at the site. The blood that oozed out came slowly, viscous. It was a deep red against his skin. Zinfandel, maybe. A Syrah, perhaps. Not a Pinot Noir.

We washed his skin with sacramental dedication.

His blood settled in his back within fifteen minutes. We turned him over and there it was, proof of his departure, the sunken parts of him no longer moving, settled there because of gravity. A freshly dead body mottles quickly. The stains spread before your eyes as if the skin was a linen draped over spilt

Merlot. We were watching our lives darken in real time.

But deliver us from evil.

I don't think anybody was the same after my brother died and I don't think anybody will ever return to who they were when he was alive. Those people are locked away, gone willingly to ferry him away. We are After Him in the timeline of the rest of our lives.

His body, when we left it, looked tiny in the adult-sized gurney. There was so much more space for him to fill. There always will be. We didn't even have his own clothes to dress him in. Walking away from that hospital room felt like stepping into another, parallel universe – we were leaving Where He Is and entering Where He Is No Longer.

–

There's a surprising amount of paperwork involved in transporting a body over state lines. I was not the one who had to make the calls and figure out how to ferry my brother back to California. That fell to my sister, a social worker. Texas Children's Hospital didn't specialize in this kind of bureaucracy and we received very little help from them with the logistics. We were all supposed to be on the same plane back to California, but more problems arose. So they shipped him in the cargo hold at the bottom of a different plane a day after us.

There's a town near San Francisco called the City of Colma. It's in the Guinness World Records for having more dead than living people. A town full of cemeteries. My great-grandmother is buried there. So is my mom's mom, who died before I was born. Tito isn't. I think he's on someone's mantel. Or maybe in the Philippines.

My brother was cremated.

He isn't in the ground somewhere. I actually know exactly

where he is. He's above our fireplace – technically. But the modern home my parents renovated doesn't exactly have a mantel. He's in a box, wrapped in an emerald green velvet bag. I don't think my parents have put him in an urn yet because it makes it seem too real. As if the tense silence of the house isn't already too real. As if all of his untouched things aren't already too real. As if all of that emptiness inside of us isn't already too real.

But before he was cremated, he was brought to Colma, to Woodlawn Funeral Home and Memorial Park. The paperwork was so screwed up they were unable to get hold of a child-sized coffin in time for his arrival. The first time I saw my small brother's body in the state where we lived, he was in a cardboard box.

He was dead. In a cardboard box.

I don't think I'll ever forget that. It's strange and hilarious in a grotesque sort of way. It's funny because it has to be funny or else it's just sad. You don't expect to see someone you love, dead at the age of ten, half-swaddled in threadbare linen, placed in a cardboard box. A shipping box. It was white on the outside. Maybe it was just sad.

A body that's been dead for a while greys. It loses the living glow and becomes ashen. Parts of the face sink and parts of the face swell, looking almost like the person you once loved, but not quite. The uncanny valley of what you once knew. And for a moment, while you're standing there, you might think, *That is not my person. Bring my person to me. Bring my person back to me alive.* But they are never brought to you and especially not alive, because that is your person and your person is dead.

His hands looked old, his dead, grey skin wrinkled at the knuckles. An entire universe of what-ifs and unknowns and might-have-beens yawned out from the wrinkled skin of his hands. What was folded in there? We would never know.

When Tito died, I went up to the coffin but I did not touch him. I couldn't; it was too weird. I remembered when Lola, my other great-grandmother, passed and they made me touch her hand. I couldn't bear to do that again. But now that my brother was in the box, I felt the compulsion. It was like I had to make sure for myself. I had to know he was dead. I had to make sure because what if this was the universe where miracles happened?

It was not the universe where miracles happened.

My sister reached across his face and did what she would do to him all the time – she pinched his nostrils. He always had a squishy nose. I smiled at it and thought that I must do it too. So I did. But his nose was not squishy. It was hard, like the plastic in children's toys. And cold, too, as if taking my body's heat for itself. I squeezed but his skin had no give. I placed my hand on his wrinkled grey ones, folded on his chest, and they were cold, stiff. I remember thinking that he felt hollow.

I will never forget the sound of the furnace they use for cremation. When it opened, it roared mechanically and there was a tinny undercurrent below the deep, bone-shaking thrum. My sister pressed the button to fire it up because nobody else volunteered. I mean, who volunteers to start the incinerator for their dead sonbrothernephew? I like that they offer the opportunity, though. Says something about finality but I'm not sure what.

–

My father never forgot that my great-grandmother did not look like herself after she was embalmed. He brought it up occasionally, like a secret he sometimes needed to tell.

At Woodlawn, before my brother arrived, we sat down with their staff to discuss options for urns and whether we were going to split his ashes between the family. We brought the dog. My parents always bring the dog around and the dog is usually a good boy, but he was an especially good boy that day.

'I can't believe we're doing this.'

My dad took his glasses off slowly and placed them on the shiny, lacquered table and the dog scooched in, putting his head on my father's lap.

The last time my dad saw my brother's body was on an adult-sized gurney in Texas Children's Hospital, and that will always be the last time.

—

After my brother's body was placed in the furnace to burn and my sister pushed the button, I walked out into the sunlight. This was in California in November, but it was still bright and warm. Or maybe it was just bright and I only think I felt warm because I actually felt nothing. I felt absence, maybe. But even now I'm not sure I felt anything.

My father was sitting on a bench as cars went up and down El Camino Real. His shoulders were slumped. He had a hat on and his head was tilted to one side, him and the dog both looking at the same nothing.

He didn't want to see what death had done to my brother's body, so he didn't. He sat outside with the dog the whole time, and a part of me wonders if he regrets not seeing his little boy one last time. But of course the answer is yes – he will always regret not seeing his little boy one last time.

He must have heard my footsteps because I didn't call out to him when I approached, but he turned his head toward me, and the dog did too, with his ears perked. In the light of day, my father's face seemed gaunt. The shadow from his hat did strange things to it, made it seem bigger in some places and smaller in others, under his eyes and by his chin. He's only forty-nine years old in this still frame of him that I carry with me now, forever. Forty-nine with two dead children and the rest who will not stop wandering the Earth and come back home.

A dying star. A black hole.

He didn't move. But when he blinked, I recall that I sighed in relief.

For thine is the kingdom, and the power, and the glory, for ever and ever.

Amen.

CALL ME BY MY NAME

I have three names: a first, a middle and a last.

I have three other names, too: my legal name, my misheard name and a name I accidentally gave myself.

My parents had three kids together and they were never in the business of finding out the sex of each foetus before the kid came crying out into the world, lungs full of air (most of us, anyway). They picked two names, a boy's name and a girl's name, and decided to match the name to our genitalia.

My mother said if I was born a boy, my name would've been Dean.

But I was named Jayne instead.

JAYNE /dʒeɪn/ *noun*:
GOD'S GIFT

It used to be one of those stupid, sleazy jokes that I would tell when I was drunk at college parties, trying to impress girls I wanted to make out with. I can see myself saying it, too, in that same stupid way every time, my smile all lopsided as if placed there by a lazy sculptor. To make it worse, I would waggle my eyebrows up and down, probably while sloshing beer around in a red cup.

My mother told me that's what my name meant: God's gift. I think she really just liked Jayne Mansfield but the meaning behind the name was a little bonus. It wasn't until I was twenty-two that my father confirmed what I'd always thought, that I was 'an accident'. He and my mother were twenty and twenty-one when they had me.

God's gift, indeed.

When I moved from San Francisco to Orange County to start high school, I became known as Jane-with-a-*y*. There was a more popular Jane in school, which surprised me – not the fact that she was more popular, but that her name was also Jane. I always felt like my name was old-fashioned, somehow. As a fourteen-year-old, I had never met another person my age who was named Jane (or Jayne, for that matter). This was the first time I ever thought about whether or not I liked my name. I was always aware that my name had an unconventional spelling, but the way my fellow students othered me from Jane seemed deliberate and, at times, maybe even malicious.

I had a crush on her, this other Jane. Which I felt odd about, sometimes. She played the violin and smiled kindly with a closed mouth, though when she laughed you could see her straight white teeth. She had delicate, slender wrists that moved the bow back and forth effortlessly, gliding across the strings with such ease, as if every part of her instrument were made of air. She was quiet and intelligent and empathic, so much so that I remember she once cried in AP biology when they had to dissect dead cats. In the spring, she wore sundresses, but during the summer she tried to limit her time in the sun, so that the pale white of her shoulders would not fleck with pigment.

I also played the violin, but I was better at the trumpet. I was loud, often shouting across campus at people I knew or teachers I had questions for. No part of me was delicate like Jane. Everything I did was boisterous and jarring, flamboyant even. I only shopped in the boys' department and had terrible posture to hide the breasts that puberty had given me.

I once met her in a park between our two homes. We sat on swing sets and she told me about her overbearing brother, about living in a strict Korean household, about church.

'Did you know our name means God's gift?' I remember asking.

She smiled, mouth closed, kind but also sad in a way.

'Yes,' she answered.

I wondered if she knew what kind of gift she was.

By the time we graduated from high school and moved to different parts of the state, I was Jayne and she was Jayne-without-a-*y*. I think this is supposed to say something about high school and growth and transformation, but I think it only says that we were and still remain very different from one another.

Months ago, I got curious and searched for her on a social media app. She's married now and has one child.

God's gift, indeed.

JAMES /dʒeɪmz/ noun:
SUPPLANTER; ONE WHO FOLLOWS

–

In 2017, I started on self-injected testosterone, a process commonly known as HRT or hormone replacement therapy. In some places, HRT specifically refers to the replacement of oestrogen in postmenopausal women. Transgender hormone therapy is often thought of as a stepping stone for 'sex reassignment surgery', a term that I think is incredibly outdated and should be referred to, in many cases (as is my own), as gender confirmation surgery.

My therapist and doctor provided me with a list of changes

I could expect, changes that could be reversed if I were to stop taking testosterone and changes that would be permanent. The list was mostly physical: muscle and fat redistribution, hair growth (or, depending on age, hair loss), voice deepening, and so on. Results may vary. Genetics may vary. Changes may vary.

It was second puberty in a vial. I experienced acne for the first time, although that sounds like bragging (and if it is, let me have this). At work, every time we had free snacks, free food, free anything that could be consumed, I was to be found. When asked what it was like, I would tell people that it was like having the appetite of a fifteen-year-old boy on the high school football team, but without the advantage of being on a football team.

I dreamed of growing facial hair, a dirty, comical moustache. Instead, I just gained weight. My shirts became too tight and my face squared out, but then started to round. Week by week my voice would stumble, crack, and then drop, as if falling down uneven steps. One week my boss took me for coffee under Rockefeller Center.

'James? I have a cortado for James?'

I looked around for who else would order a cortado, but nobody moved. I made awkward eye contact with the barista who still had the drink in his hand.

'James?' he said, louder, looking directly at me.

I accepted the beverage with an apology.

'What if I changed my name to Kevin?' I once asked my father. His name is Kevin, which we joke is an incredibly boring name for a human but an incredibly interesting name for a dog.

'All the names on Earth and you'd pick Kevin?'

No, I would not pick Kevin. He did not offer up any alternatives.

My mother has taken to sending me photos of myself with long hair and glasses, breasts I can't stand to look at, clothes that never fit me quite right. I think she misses this version of me that

I try not to associate myself with anymore. But I can't tell her to stop because I think it would upset her. It would make her feel like I killed her daughter.

'Are you thinking of changing your name?' my mother asked me.

'No,' I said. At the time, I was not sure that it was the truth.

She backtracked and said I could do what I want but she had always liked my name. *Yes*, I thought, *that's why you picked it*.

When I make reservations or order coffee or pick up my takeaway order they somehow never have an order for Jayne, but they do always have an order for James. Once, because of the confusion, I had to laugh and say that my girlfriend placed the order and I didn't know which name she'd given – mine or hers. Mine or hers. But her name is Emily and neither of us are named James.

I hate making people uncomfortable.

'James?'

I always look toward the voice of inquiry before I move. Whoever asks for James makes eye contact with me, and only when they smile do I take a step forward. James is not my name, but it is the name they call me anyway. It's the name they want to hear, the person they want to ask for.

And when they ask for him, I reply.

JACK /dʒak/ noun:
GOD IS GRACIOUS; SUPPLANTER

On 10 July 2018, I had a bilateral mastectomy.

Top surgery was one of those things that I had wanted for years. My breasts caused me a deep and often indescribable discomfort. I was a late bloomer. When I was fourteen, I could still laughingly click together the shoulder straps of my backpack because I was so flat chested. And then, very suddenly, I was not.

And then, very suddenly, I was again.

The night before my mastectomy, I texted Emily.

'I think I'm scared,' I said. 'But I'm not sure.'

I had never had major surgery. I'd never been put under general anaesthesia. I read horror stories of patients suddenly regaining consciousness in the middle of their own surgery, locked in their body while repair and extraction took place. I wasn't allergic to any medication, but what if I was allergic to anaesthetic drugs? I was scared of the surgery. What if I went to sleep and didn't wake up? Would I even know if I had died? I wondered if there is a moment before death when we think, *This is it. I am dying.* Do we know when we leave?

I never even got to the part where they put the mask on me. The last thing I remember was the nurse pulling up the side railing on my gurney so they could move me to the operating room. Apparently, the last thing I said to the friend who took me to my surgery was 'loved one', before I disappeared behind a swinging door.

That was at 8 a.m. I woke up at 2 p.m. wondering where my glasses and my friend were.

'You need your glasses that badly, honey?' my nurse asked me.

'Yes,' I croaked. I had a tube in my throat for hours. 'So I can see if there are any cute nurses around.'

When I finally got my glasses back and my friend was called for, I asked the nurse assigned to me what her name was. She handed me a popsicle for my throat. It was strawberry flavoured.

'My name is Jayne, spelled just like yours,' she said, smiling. She had an Australian accent.

In my post-operation, drug-addled state, I remembered questioning if she were real. I still have my discharge papers, signed by Nurse Jayne. She gave me four more popsicles and made sure I didn't faint before I got dressed and went home. I tried to stay awake in the passenger seat while my friend – the 'loved one' –

drove me. I made it about halfway before I went back to sleep.

Before my surgery I signed up for a gym and went six days a week for ten weeks to try and work off some of the weight I'd gained after starting testosterone. My surgeon had said slimming down would improve my surgery results. It was tough, slow work that reminded me of starting on testosterone. I wanted results immediately, but bodies have other plans. I did cardio – hours and hours of running on the treadmill – because I was afraid of the free weights even though I had spent money for a gym membership for the idea of free weights. My body shifted gradually. But it did shift.

I'm not very athletic even though I was a full-time athlete as an undergraduate. I was the coxswain for our rowing team. I played recreational dodgeball in New York City. For a short stint one winter I ran, and counted dogs as motivation, on frosty mornings in Prospect Park in Brooklyn. But I don't know how to work out, really. I prefer something or someone to tell me what to do and exactly how to do it. During those ten weeks, I just ran on the treadmill, no guidance except my self-imposed rule of getting off only when the machine said I'd burned 500 calories. I enjoy numbers. I like quantifiable evidence of progress.

I lost a substantial amount of weight leading up to my surgery and then . . . well, and then I wasn't able to work out for a while. No pushing, no pulling, no lifting things heavier than a gallon of milk, not until my surgeon cleared me for physical activity. That clearance didn't happen until August, and on 1 September, I moved to Dublin, Ireland, to pursue my master's in creative writing. The frustration of muscle atrophy and the thought of sitting and writing for lengthy periods convinced me to promise myself to join an athletics team so that I could have a programme to follow.

When I was on the rowing team in college, I was on the women's rowing team. It made sense given my gender marker and identity at the time. Even though I presented differently from most people on the team, I was happy to be on it. So it was different when I went to the sports centre to sign up after my bilateral mastectomy, after being on testosterone for over a year. On the one hand, the women's team; on the other, the men's.

I am five feet four inches tall, which is average for a woman and short for a man and even shorter for an athletic man. I don't identify as man or woman (or the elusive third gender, athletic man), but there aren't many places for non-binary athletes. I asked the man at the rowing booth how much it cost to join the team and when practices were. He needed my student ID card to sign me up.

I hesitated.

Originally, I hadn't planned on telling them that I was not a man. I wanted to go, work out, maybe compete, and then leave quietly after my one-year programme was finished. But there are always unforeseen moments when we must out ourselves in society. And this was just one of them.

'I . . . wasn't born a man,' I said, with my student ID card hanging in the air between us. 'And I don't want to be a coxswain.'

He looked surprised but didn't say much when he entered in my information. I thought I felt the heads of others turn to look at me when I spoke but I like to think that they minded their own business, that the gym – at that time – was so loud they could not hear me out myself. I like to think that I am so unimportant that my transness slips out of my mouth like a sigh and goes unnoticed.

I like to think that because to think otherwise feels dangerous to me.

Before our first practice on the water, we had to pass a swim test with the university. I dreaded it. When I was a kid, my parents enrolled me in swim lessons. I loved the pool, until I didn't. I started to dislike the pool because I hated the one-piece swimsuit and the thought of putting my body into it. I love the beach, but I wore a T-shirt over every pair of board shorts and swim trunks I owned. I had surgery in the summer and the only soaking I was allowed to do was one night in a bathtub with my partner, who patiently, carefully, washed my hair and laughed when she got shampoo in my eyes anyway.

I wished so desperately that she was there when I had to take the swim test.

It seemed unfair that she wasn't. That I couldn't share this milestone with her. It's such a stupid, tiny thing and yet I had to do it. I had to get in a pair of swim trunks at a public pool and for the first time, I would not have a top on.

The team captain who was supposed to be supervising was not there. The lifeguard told me she'd take my name down, proof that I had been there.

'Just down the lane once is fine,' she said, waving her hand casual-like.

My big moment, my big reveal, reduced to 'down the lane once'. Unlike the conversation in the gym, I felt like I wanted to be noticed. I felt like I wanted somebody to congratulate me. Even if it was just my partner. Especially if it was just my partner. But it was only me and the casual lifeguard on duty, and when I texted my partner afterward, she asked me how I felt.

I almost wish that I had felt more. But it felt like I had just participated in someone else's moment. A glimpse into someone else's everyday life. I couldn't tell if that was a good or bad thing.

I intended to pass as a man on the rowing team. I really thought that I could have just gone in, done my work, and gotten out. I didn't exactly think the whole thing through, really, I just wanted something for myself, something I knew I could already do, had already done. If anybody asked me, I was just a guy. A guy named James.

'How you gettin' on?' The kid was probably ten years younger than me and about eight inches taller. He seemed nice enough but when I asked him his name, he stuck his hand out and shook my own. 'Name's James. Yourself?'

'Jack,' I said, almost fumbling with the syllable in my mouth. Because instead of commenting on the odd absurdity of James being both of our names, my brain did a very rational thing and sought to instantly run through a shortlist of other *j* names to rename myself. It settled on Jack. James probably showed up to half a dozen practices before he never returned and I kept showing up as Jack.

JAYNE /dʒeɪn/ noun:
GOD IS GRACIOUS

The very first practice we had on the water, I couldn't unknow what I already knew about rowing. I took one stroke and the coach stopped me.

'I thought you said you hadn't done this before.'

'I lied.'

It wasn't technically a lie. I had no racing experience as a rower; I was only a coxswain. But they were concerned about my eligibility to race at novice level since I did technically have prior experience.

'They wouldn't be able to find any record of me, even if they did,' I said. 'I was on a women's team. And I had a different name.'

'Well, there's certainly a first time for everything,' the coach said.

After that, there was only one guy who misgendered me, called me 'she' every time he saw me. I couldn't tell if it was malicious; nobody else who had been there that day had any problem. I like to think that people aren't malicious, that maybe he just wasn't as bright as the others, but I guess I'll never know.

He ended up quitting quite early on.

I got asked if I played American football. A guy roughhoused with me in the way that boys do. For ten days, I went to training camp with them in Seville, Spain. They never called me anything other than Jack. Jack was my name for as long as I was on that team. It was like immersive training for how to be a boy every time I went to a practice. My life as Dean, the name my mother would have given me had I been born a boy, seemed to wax and wane before me like a mirage in the desert, sometimes close enough to touch. Who I was as Jayne did not come onto the bus with me on the way to the river or through the doors of the gym. I played pretend as a man named Jack.

I was not a man named Jack.

Just like I was not a man named James.

I had drinks one night with the team and one of the ladies from the women's crew got to talking to me about being not-Jack.

'I was there,' she said. 'At the table, when you signed up.'

She said that she heard me when I said I wasn't born a man, that I had been on the women's team before. She remembered me from that time I outed myself in the loud gymnasium, the time I thought that the only people who were in on my conversation were myself and the man who had read my student ID card. That moment that I thought – that I hoped – was private was stored inside someone else's memory. I wondered who else had heard, who else knew that I was not a man on the rowing team whose name was Jack. Who looked at me and knew that I was not who I said I was?

When I went to the immigration office nearly three months after arriving in Dublin, the man who took my passport looked at it and still called me 'sir'. At Seville, we had to give our passports to reception, in case anything went wrong with our rooms. On the last day, one of the senior guys made a big show of giving back everyone's documents – an attempt to embarrass all by exposing their young, fresh-faced photos; but when he got to me, he quietly handed mine back without much fanfare. At the gym on campus, I ask to use the changing rooms for the pool, because they have individual stalls. When they lock entry for students for a special event, I tell them about my special case: 'I am a transgender student,' I say apologetically.

I thought about the swim test that I had to take. Did someone notice me then? Did someone see my scars and think, *How brave!* But I never feel brave. I have only felt scared. I want to be seen and unseen, always wanting to just be and be acknowledged for being. *Look at me,* I think, *but please never too closely. Notice me, but only if you are kind.*

That lap I swam down the pool was the first lap I'd swum in years. I felt the slight tug and stretch of my scars as I went down the lane, freestyle. It took a few strokes for me to remember how to breathe, to remember how to move through the water, cutting down the pool in a straight line. My mouth and nose filled with water and I felt pressure to do this quickly, though the pressure was only internal. I slowed down and swam leisurely, trying not to overdo it for my cardiovascular health. The world fell away and I remembered what I liked so much about swimming, about exercise – the awareness of my body as mine, controlled by me, working for me. My body was mine, finally.

The name Jane does not mean 'God's gift'. Or at least, the name means 'God is gracious'. In a way, the name means that God presents a gift and that the person who is named Jane is the gift. I never thought I was much of a gift, nor was I proof that God was particularly gracious.

But I finally feel present.

Before I started on testosterone, there were a few instances of a misplaced name. Usually it was in a loud bar, or sometimes I was presenting in a much more masculine manner, but it was pretty typical to hear me introduce myself as 'Jayne, like Tarzan and . . .' while people filled in the rest. At bars or clubs, women would be so amused by my introduction they would start calling me Tarzan. I like to think they were amused, anyway. It seems better than any alternative. But today I have to introduce myself differently.

People still hear James because they would much rather hear James, because it's more comfortable for them to hear James. James matches what they see with what they want to hear. But my name is not James. Nor is it Jack.

'My name is Jayne, like the woman's name,' I say, but Jayne is not a woman's name, either. It's my name. And I am not a woman. For some people, it's enough clarity that they don't question my parents' mistake in naming me. I do not enjoy introducing myself that way, as if my name is ill-fitting, as if 'the woman's name' is a mistake I must come to live with and make everyone accept. Or like it's a joke and now we are both in on the punchline, this joke of my name. I introduce myself that way so there is no confusion as to what my name is, because it's easier for other people if I acknowledge the absurdity of my name before they do. I do not enjoy introducing myself that way, but I do it anyway.

Years ago, after I had come out as non-binary, someone who didn't know me prior to coming out, prior to transitioning, asked me if I chose my name. There's a character in one of my favourite sci-fi shows who's a space mercenary. He has an entire episode dedicated to a small part of his backstory and in that episode you learn that he is 'The hero of Canton, the man they call Jayne' because his name was, like the nurse after my surgery, Jayne. This person thought I had chosen my name because of that character.

And I told this person the name Jayne was given to me by my parents, like most people.

Years afterward, I realize the small irony of the question.

Every day, I choose my name. My name is not James and it is not Jack. It is not a woman's name, nor a man's name. It is not a dead name, for no part of me has died. It is a birth name, because my parents gave it to me at birth. It's the name I grew into, the name I've become present in. The name I've inhabited more gladly than any other name I've been called. It's the name on my birth certificate and passport and social security card. It's the name in my partner's phone, followed by a little heart – the name she says when she calls me long distance.

I've been called Jack and James. I've been expected to answer to those names and I have been obliging. But those names are not my name. They are not me. They are not my identity. My name was both given to me and chosen by me.

My name is Jayne. Please, call me by my name.

A BODY IN MOTION

The way my partner feels about my body is something I don't understand.

I can't understand how she finds me attractive. On a logical level, I understand that beauty is in the eye of the beholder, that our tastes are not the tastes of others. But on a personal and emotional level, I find it hard to believe because I have never seen myself as attractive. I have never loved myself in the way that marketing trends and self-care advice say you are supposed to love yourself. I don't understand how to.

My partner does it for me anyway.

Hating your body is hardly revolutionary. Every person I've had a meaningful conversation with about the body has felt some amount of dislike toward their own. It's possible every single one of us has looked in the mirror and disliked what we saw: too much fat in the hips, the thighs, the arms, too skinny in the calves or the ankles, not toned enough, shoulders too broad, hips too narrow, zits, scars, stretch marks, hairlines, nail beds, follicles, tits, biceps, beards . . . the list is endless. A checklist of imperfections.

It seems like an integral part of the human experience – to dislike something about ourselves – that people find it very easy to draw up false equivalences when trying to compare their issues of self-image with the experience of body dysphoria in people like me.

'I mean, I hate what I see in the mirror, I can only imagine how painful it must be for you!'

Trying to understand a trans person's feelings toward their body is impossible by that route. These statements are well-meaning, but ill-informed misinterpretations of dysphoria and dysphoric thoughts. I understand that for many cisgender people, that is how it must be. That the self-hate must be so intense the only solution to the 'problem' is medically sanctioned self-mutilation.

Typing these words is painful. Having to reiterate the misconception is difficult.

I did not change my body because I hated myself so much that I wished to cause myself harm. That's the rhetoric I hear, the undercurrent of what happens when people discuss the bodies of transmen and transwomen and trans people without our voices. No, I did not change my body because I hated myself.

I changed my body because of what little love I could muster for it.

Medically transitioning made sense to me. I knew it would help me on my journey to love myself better – but medical transition is not the be-all and end-all for every trans person. It's not the only path for this journey, which sometimes does not have an end. We are never just befores and afters of ourselves; we are all – cis and trans – constantly improving and changing and in progress. The part of me that wanted to love myself, that wanted to understand what that love was like, knew, through no small amount of professional therapy and introspection, that hormones and surgery were what I wanted for myself, what I wanted for a future self, a self that could, perhaps, love the body I was in.

—

When I was a kid and my parents were still together, my dad would work on his brilliantly red, incredibly loud 1966 Chevelle in the garage and I would attempt to help him. I'm not sure I was of any help, if I knew then the difference between the various wrenches, screwdrivers and pliers. I only remember that I wanted to help him, with the hope that I was becoming like him.

I wanted so much to be like my father that one day, when he went to work on the car with his shirt off, I went to go work on the car with my shirt off too. My mother reprimanded me for it – girls did not do things with their shirts off. Only boys could do that.

I can't remember how old I was, but I remember the anger I felt. The nature of my childish anger, the temper tantrum, was not because girls weren't allowed to have their shirts off; it was because I was not a boy.

My father still has the car, though it's been many years since it's been driven. It's completely gutted and stripped of paint; a brand-new engine-block sits near the car's body. That brilliant red is gone, sanded down to a white primer. Even the interior is completely dismantled. Is the steering wheel still attached? I'm not sure. The car sits in pieces in the garage.

Many cis people say that they cannot imagine what it must feel like to be trapped in a body that they hate. They are trying to understand my experience in extrapolated terms with which they govern their own bodies. But my body is not their body. They're imagining things wrongly. They are still hung up on the problem of the gender binary. That trans people must have something inherently wrong with their bodies and that is what makes them trans.

They think the problem is ourselves. And yes, dysphoria is a problem within ourselves that we feel about ourselves, but sometimes dysphoria is as much an external pain as an internal one. Sometimes we know exactly who we are. We dismantle ourselves, take ourselves apart and try to put ourselves back together again so that our vision for ourselves is clear to the people around us.

My father did not take that car apart because he hated it; he took it apart with all the love and intention of putting it back together to be better than it was before.

–

My partner waits for me outside of gendered restrooms. She tells me that she gets nervous for me when I disappear behind the door marked for men. When I come out of the bathroom, flapping my hands dry in the air, she smiles at me as if I've just came out of the arrivals gate at an airport.

If the restroom is gendered, I am always using the wrong one.

Sometimes, there's a bathroom that's unisex. More often than not, however, it's also the only one outfitted to assist a disabled person. I think about using those bathrooms a lot and sometimes I do, but as someone who's able-bodied, who only needs to sit to pee, I think that there are others who might be in more dire need of that bathroom than I. It's strange to be almost pitted against disabled people for bathroom use. Like we have to wait and queue against one another.

These stalls do provide a certain amount of safety, but it's a different kind of safety we want for our bodies than those who might need the extra railings or wider space. It feels as if we're presented with a choice – our safety or someone else's. What we need is the safety of not being confronted with being in the 'wrong' place. But we are in the wrong space when we occupy a particular stall that someone else is waiting for, which has the aids they need to do their business.

We all just want to do our business, mind our own business, conduct our business in private. But these are public spaces. It's never just about us, is it? It's about everyone else around us. Other people get to determine if we are in the right place, based on how we look or how well we 'pass'.

Are we ever in the right place?

Or are we only in the right place when we are alone?

–

My decision to medically transition was, at first, a reluctant one.

I didn't know of all the changes testosterone would bring. After all, I had spent a lot of time telling myself and others that I was comfortable in my femininity. I thought that meant comfortable in my female body, despite my expression of gender through my clothes. I am comfortable in my femininity today, but only because I now understand what feminine means to me. In the years leading up to my transition, feminine felt . . . girly, pink, light and airy. But those are not the only things that feminine can mean.

Many trans people and gender non-conforming folks agree that they express their gender through their clothes. For me, it was more about how I was perceived in those clothes than about wearing what I wanted. When folks talk about using clothes as a way of expressing themselves, I feel a little disconnected. It's not that I don't understand the concept, but my clothes were never an extension of my self. They were something I wore so others could see me the way I wanted to be seen, a tool I used. I wanted to be seen – and I wanted to be seen in a certain way, through a certain lens.

I wore clothes so that people would see me as less straight, less traditional, less heteronormative. I wanted to be seen as queer. At the beginning of my college career, being queer felt as much a part of my personality as it did my identity. Queer as a personality trait is something entirely different than queer as an aspect of identity. A queer identity is the lens through which one sees the world. Queer as a personality trait is making sure that that is the first thing people know about me, the forceful shaping of others' lenses on me. Their acknowledgement of my queerness was not just a validation but the lifeblood of social interactions. That they perceive my queerness was as important as understanding that I was queer.

My queerness was my masculinity. My queerness was my non-traditional existence as an Asian-American – I felt that my heritage and my sexuality did not coexist happily at that time. I made very deliberate choices to be seen and observed as something different than what I thought people knew to be a 'typical Asian'. I wanted to be seen as masculine, but I thought that I was comfortable in whatever perceived notions of womanhood people wanted to associate with me.

I was 'she' and 'her' because I did not know any other way to be.

And then I discovered the wide world of 'they' and 'them' and it felt, in all manner of cliché, like coming home. Like settling into something uniquely my own, tailormade. Like existing comfortably without the weight of being perceived by others.

This felt like the right place for me. 'They' and 'them' felt like answers to a question that I wasn't fully aware I was asking. Whether or not people adopted the use of pronouns was something I was willing to take on, because even without other people to tell me what was right or wrong in my identity, putting on 'they' and 'them' felt like a rightness I could not ignore. Something impeccable, almost. Something so precise, it felt as if I had turned a puzzle piece that *almost just* fit and for the first time, it really did. Those pronouns were extensions of myself in ways that my clothes could never properly be.

Even if I was alone, even if nobody would call me what I wanted to be called, even if they would not see me as what I knew I was, that was almost fine.

Are we only in the right place when we are alone?

No. But alone or not, the right place is there for us when we find it.

–

I asked my dad what colour he was going to repaint the Chevelle.

I'd assumed that he was just going to go back over it with that same, memorable, bright red – the kind of colour only women in movies wear. He told me that there was this kind of plum colour the Chevelle was originally painted in. I didn't know that it had been anything but fire-truck red.

In photos of hot rods, I always gravitate toward the ones with racing stripes. I love those solid swathes of bold colour running from nose to tail. I asked if he'd ever put racing stripes on the old Chevelle, but he told me that it was uncommon for a Chevelle to have racing stripes.

'I think racing stripes would be cool on the Chevelle,' I told my dad.

–

Whenever somebody asks me how many tattoos I have, I count them before I can answer. I can't really remember – I don't keep track. At the time of writing, I have nine, with a tenth planned. They vary in size and shape; one took twenty minutes, another took seven and a half hours. One is just a word, another is entirely plants.

I started getting tattoos as tributes to other people, people who were no longer in this world. When I was nineteen, this seemed like a perfectly valid reason to start getting tattoos. I wanted one as soon as I turned eighteen, but my mother said I needed to wait a year, and if I still wanted that tattoo then, I could get it. I no longer need to ask for her permission to get tattoos. I think she quite likes the ones I have these days.

My second tattoo, two years after the first, was also a tribute to someone. It took me another three years to get my third tattoo, finally a tribute to myself. After that, the amount of time between tattoos got shorter, especially when it became apparent that I was going to go the route of medically assisted transition.

I like to think that paying to have art inked permanently on my body is another way I am able to exert control over the thing I have to reside in for the rest of my life. Pushing forward on testosterone along with the acquisition of bigger, better tattoos, felt like I had given myself permission to finally become the person I'd always wanted to be. I love messaging the right artist for my next piece, the conversations we have and the designs they come up with. By permanently altering my body with ink, I find that I get closer and closer to the idea of who I want to be when I grow up.

So many queer people have tattoos and I wonder if it's the same for them. In a society and culture where we are already so othered, it only makes sense that we take advantage of our otherness and claim our physical features. Getting tattoos makes me feel as if I'm completely in control of how others see my body.

My dad's Chevelle sits unpainted, still in the garage, still in pieces, but loved so dearly. It'll get put back together one day; I'll make sure of it. Whether or not it has racing stripes, though, is something I'll leave to my dad. He likes the thought of restoring the Chevelle to its classic, old-school cool. But maybe he thought of my tattoos when he shrugged about the car.

'Yeah,' he said. 'If I'm paying, I can make it look however I want.'

–

I never fully accepted that getting top surgery – getting my breasts removed – was a medical procedure.

Which I'm sure sounds stupid.

Top surgery was something I'd wanted my entire life, something I had always thought would make my life better. But I didn't see it as a medical procedure, because I didn't see myself as a transgender person. I had internalized transphobia; I thought being transgender was shameful and something that only people who truly hated themselves identified as. I just wanted to have my breasts removed. I was not transgender and because of that, I did not think of the procedure as an exclusively transgender one. It was not a stage in my transition because I had wanted it before I thought of myself as transitioning or a body in transition.

Some people come out, either in their sexuality or their gender identity, and say that they have always known. I never felt that way in any of my coming out process. I always felt like I had to stumble upon the discovery, try it on in a dressing room to make sure that it fit properly, and then wear it out. I realize now that I have always done things to assuage those dysphoric feelings before I could properly unpack what those feelings meant.

I wanted the procedure because I hated my breasts, but I didn't want it because I hated myself. Too often I have read the misconception that transgender people who turn to medically assisted transition are participating in acts of self-mutilation. A twisted logic. To them, it seems like the procedures and the shots and all of it aren't worth the supposed payoff. They lack a level of understanding that I cannot begin to impart to them.

I only know how to tell the story my way.

And my way was this: I wanted to love myself so much, so fiercely, that I was willing to do whatever I could so that I would not keep hating the person I was forced to be seen as.

My top surgery feels like the only thing I ever did to save my own life. Some days it feels like the one act of self-love I have ever fully committed to.

I have spent much of my life convincing myself that I was too much or not enough, a paradox of amalgamations both too big and too small for what I saw as me. I am intimately aware of what self-hatred feels like. I've thought and said many bad things about myself but transitioning and using modern medicine to do it are not among those bad things.

I was lucky to get top surgery when I did. I had help and guidance, and people reassuring me and making sure every step toward my surgery was complete.

Nobody convinced me to do anything I didn't want to do. At no point in the entire process did I feel like I was doing something that was not in my best interests. It did not feel like self-mutilation, self-harm, or medically assisted, self-inflicted trauma. It felt like the right path toward becoming a person who could finally learn to love themselves.

Today, I recognize that my bilateral double mastectomy was indeed a medical procedure. In the days leading up to it, I recognized it as a medical procedure. But it took time for me to call it that because I had always considered surgeries to be urgent extrications of disease. They were always about removal, about whittling and taking away, cutting up and taking out, and I didn't associate that with the removal of my breast tissue because it seemed like a natural solution. My surgery was both removal and a way to mitigate dysphoria, but that was only a fraction of it.

The majority of surgery is healing.

My procedure took somewhere around three to four hours. Healing took six to eight weeks. But the emotional strength that I gained from going through all of that . . . that's still something I'm processing. That's something I will process for a long time.

–

I like to tease my partner because she had a crush on me for a long time before we started dating. I like to look at her when we are quiet and alone and ask her, 'Tell me again how you liked me before.' I say teasing but it's not, not really.

My partner and I met when we were both in college, seven years before we started dating. She never knew me with long hair, but she did know me with breasts, before testosterone, before my voice dropped and I developed a disappointing stubble above my upper lip. She knew me before 'they' and 'them', before queer. She met me as 'she' and 'her', as a lesbian, as a woman.

I really, truly believed that I was not loveable or desirable as a body in transition.

I thought about the times I'd been told I was in the wrong bathroom or the difficulties people had when they told me that 'they' and 'them' were pronouns used for groups of people, not a single person. I thought about the times people corrected themselves when they said 'sir' or 'ma'am' or 'miss', swinging like an apologetic pendulum between one and the others and back again. These things that I experienced, I felt that I had to experience them alone. I felt that taking somebody on this journey would be unfair to them. I sometimes placed a target on myself just by going out into the world. How could I do that to someone else?

I thought that, even if I ended up alone, I needed to do these things and identify this way because that's who I was. It wasn't something I tried on – it was a truth that I needed to live or else I would die.

I wanted to find that right place and live in it, even if that meant I lived a single and solitary existence.

But my partner found a way to love me through all that change.

I ask her all the time, selfishly, greedily, hungrily: how did this all happen? How did we happen?

She met me at what some people would call a before. And she remains with me at what some people would call an after. I am not a before and an after. I feel that I am still very much in transition, that there are still things about myself I'm learning to claim and learning to love, and I do not know if there is an end to that. Sometimes we settle where we are comfortable. And sometimes we keep going, just to explore. Sometimes the road doesn't stop.

My partner decided to take her chances with me just a month before my top surgery date. We were friends for a long time before that, but the tender-heartedness with which she helped me through my recovery was something entirely different. And it wasn't just that I was recovering from a medical procedure; it wasn't only the obligation of a new relationship through adversity. My partner wanted to be with me at this tumultuous time in my life. I couldn't help but fall as fast as I did. I was so grateful.

But she did not need me to be grateful. She only wanted to love me. In whatever iteration of self I presented to her.

—

My partner showed me such love when she helped me recover and she has showed me that same kind of love every day since. It's only through her example that I'm able to recognize and acknowledge that the things that I did for myself weren't acts of self-mutilation: they were acts of self-love.

Whenever I see arguments about trans people made by people who do not identify as trans, I wonder what their radical acts of self-love are. I wonder if they love themselves so much that they would save their own lives if they could. I imagine that they would. I imagine that most people try to muster up enough love for themselves to make it through one day on toward the next, even if that's all they can manage at the time. I imagine that their radical acts of self-love sometimes require the scary step of asking someone else for help.

I asked for help. That first someone else was a gender therapist. And then, after, a general physician.

Being transgender doesn't necessarily mean that I hate my body. I have hated my body, this is true – but this is not exclusive to the transgender experience. The acute sense that I have of my body and all the ways that it was not mine until I did the things that I did, does not make my experience a uniquely transgender experience. Nor does my decision to participate in medically assisted transition make my experience a transgender one.

I cannot say what makes a person's experience a transgender one.

I only know that mine is.

I said that I have never loved myself the way that I am supposed to, but I am only able to write this because eventually I did. I did love myself, ardently and fiercely, enough to want to save my own life. I loved myself the way we are supposed to love people who are struggling to heal from wounds that we cannot see – we help them recover.

Against godliness

. . . quanto la cosa è più perfetta,
più senta il bene, e così la doglienza.

. . . the more perfect a thing is
the more it feels of pleasure and of pain.

— Virgil to Dante in the *Divine Comedy*

I. Lust

I was always wanting.

When I decided to transition, it was through a series of wants. I wanted things. I wanted change. I thought about what I could gain rather than what I hoped to lose. But I wanted before that, too. I wanted before I decided. I was always wanting, though I rarely felt wanted.

—

I was an awkward teenager. There was something about my sense of humour or the way I approached groups of people that wasn't quite right. Perhaps a large part of my awkwardness was because

I did not possess the typical social anxieties of people my age. My parents, young when they had me, encouraged me to talk to adults as if I was an adult; otherwise, who else was I to interact with? If I were to paint myself in the best light, with all the advantages offered by hindsight, I'd say that I was more emotionally mature than others. I grew faster than others. My awkwardness was not because I didn't know how to communicate, but because I didn't approach conversations with the same hesitation as my peers. I was overeager, and that eagerness to chat, to befriend, that's what was awkward.

I went to college and joined a sports team and suddenly there was this girl. She was tall. They all were – gorgeous, skin kissed by the Southern Californian sun. Their year-round tans were the result of good genetics and geographical privilege. If I have a type, it's because I live in a society that upholds a certain kind of beauty standard and possibly because this girl may very well be the originator of my type, ground zero for my preference for blonde white women. Describing her as conventionally attractive feels wrong, but it's not untrue. She was, and is, conventionally attractive from a Western, specifically American, point of view.

Her hair was always varying shades of blonde – never going so far as platinum but not straying too far into brunette either. As somebody who was neither blonde, nor tall, I often thought to myself, *How could I not be attracted to her?* We were so different. She is white with green eyes, skin that freckles when she's out in the sun too much. I am short, both Chinese and Filipino, and my skin craves the sun so much that when I am not in it, I look ill. I was not meant to live in places with real winters. We are visual juxtapositions; if we were a Venn diagram, our only intersecting physical trait would be the bronze we got from the sun.

This person, who I now call one of my best friends, was not a conquest. This is not an anecdote about 'the friendzone', nor a sob story about how we did not fall in love and run off together into that Southern Californian sunset. I was always so hurt that this hilarious, intelligent, and beautiful woman could not see me as a potential suitor. I did not see myself as being entitled to her. But I felt a real hurt that I could not, in whatever capacity, be chosen by her.

It was more about me than it was about her. As much as I wanted her, desired her, pined for her, I really just wanted to be somebody who she would want. I wanted to be somebody who someone like her would date, or even spare a glance at. I wanted to be the kind of person who could be with somebody like her. Writing this many years after these feelings have dissipated, I know that the hurt I felt, that real ache, was an extension of my own self-criticism and negative self-image. I wanted to be someone who I was not. Someone she could want.

At the time, I thought that meant someone who was a man.

Today, we both know that isn't true.

–

Wanting somebody makes them a part of you, a part of your story. That desire, that pining, that becomes a chapter in our lives, even if the desire is unrequited. Even if that person has no idea you desire them, we conflate them with our own narrative. They are given a recurring role, sometimes. Or a speaking part, maybe.

Testosterone made me want other people in a way and with a frequency I had never experienced before. The first month on hormones, I wanted every beautiful body I passed pressed up against me. How could this tiny vial of viscous oil-like substance make me crave people in a way that felt animalistic?

This is *not* an excuse for rape culture, for 'boys will be boys', for 'he does that because he likes you', for 'men have urges that need to be satisfied'. I wanted people so much more than I had before, but it didn't make me feel out of control in my body. It didn't make the wanting feel like something I had to act on. It didn't make me more impulsive or more likely to do things to other people. I wanted with greater frequency but at the same distance.

Before transition and during, I wanted so much but never felt desired. I had opportunities to date while I was going through this deeply personal journey, but how could I drag someone along with me? It felt selfish, almost, to want someone and to not be lonely while wanting change for myself.

It was impossible for me to feel that somebody would choose to be with me. It was unthinkable. I desired every manner of body and shape and personality but, before my transition and during, I never felt that I was the desirable one. I thought I had to reach the finish line of change. I had to obtain those neat, simple before and after photos – my proof of change. In order for people to find me desirable, I had to present myself as a finished product.

But I had no idea what my 'finished' product was. Nor did I really believe there was an end.

–

II. GLUTTONY

When I was a child, my parents were not as well off as they are today. I never went hungry, but like most children of immigrants, I grew up with a certain appreciation for and feeling of obligation around food. We never turned down food from our elders and we always cleared our plates. I find this to be true across all diasporas. We must not waste.

My partner, who is white, did not quite understand this.

Early in our relationship, we went to lunch with my family and, shortly after, my stepfather, whose family is originally from Mexico, went to his parents' home to drop something off. He came back with a plate of ribs and beans that we picked at and ate while standing at the counter.

'Didn't we just have lunch?' my partner asked. Intellectually, she knew that food and being offered food was an important part of immigrant culture but she hadn't quite seen it in practice, where the amount of time between meals doesn't matter when family offers you food.

If there is food on a plate, you must eat. And that's how I eat today.

–

My father is a great cook. He enjoys cooking, especially for other people, and the experience of eating, even if it will cost a premium. My mother has gotten better at cooking in recent years, but she does not enjoy cooking for other people. She's self-conscious about it and would prefer to bring people to a good deal in a restaurant rather than cook for them.

I understand this to be the reverse in most families, that mothers are the ones who cook and fathers are the ones who go to restaurants or get takeout. I guess my family roles don't adhere to the binary either.

My father learned to cook because he wanted to eat well. He wanted to eat good food, food from around the world, food from different cultures, food he couldn't afford to buy. He couldn't always afford the convenience of takeaway meals, restaurants or even fast-food joints. If he wanted to eat, and to eat good food, he had to make it himself.

When I left home and went to college, I felt the same. I

wanted to eat good food, food from around the world, food from different cultures, food I couldn't afford to buy. But the cafeteria and dining commons on a college campus didn't exactly provide a diverse menu for its student population. And the amount of money that I made while working at said dining commons wasn't enough to buy lavish meals.

So I watched cooking shows and YouTube chefs. I sat on the couches of my college apartments and watched Food Network as I ate.

–

Second puberty was different from the first, mostly because I was aware that it was happening to me, and partly because it manifested itself in diffcrent ways than the first. Second puberty made me want to eat any kind of food, all the time. I didn't care about eating well and the food was often not delicious.

I had the appetite of a high school football player. But I had a sedentary office job with an hour-long commute on either side of the workday and very little of that commute involved moving my legs. I consumed shamelessly and with little thought or care. I just wanted – needed – to eat.

I was warned, of course, that this was going to be a side effect of taking testosterone. But they said that my appetite would possibly increase, not that my hunger would become intense and insatiable. Food was no longer a gateway to appreciating the way other cultures spiced, presented and cooked ingredients. It was no longer a path of learning, and the thought and care that went into the art of cooking was no longer important. I was not interested in the diasporas of different people when I ate.

I was only worried about still being hungry.

–

My appetite eventually died down, but I'm not sure if it was the heat of the summer, the natural progression of my body's hormones regulating themselves, or any other of the number of changes that occurred around the time my wide-open mouth started to shut. The effects of my unrestrained appetite left visible marks on my body, mostly on my gut and chin.

After starting testosterone I'm not sure how much weight I gained in total, but I think at my heaviest, it was nearly 45 lbs. When I was finally approved for top surgery, my surgeon urged me to lose weight, telling me that the best results would occur when I was more fit and closer to my ideal weight.

I had to learn the meaning of eating well, yet again.

And this time, it wasn't just the reverse of what had caused me to balloon outward. I couldn't just eat less; I had to eat less of some things and more of others. Less meat, more veggies. It was supposed to be simple, but it took me much, much longer to work off that weight than it did for me to eat up to it. It took a lot of work, but in preparation for my bilateral double mastectomy, I got back down to the weight I was prior to starting testosterone.

These days, I get a blood test once a year, to make sure my hormone levels are regular. One of my cholesterol levels is a mild concern. It's not a huge concern, but still. It's enough to make sure that I keep eating well.

—

III. GREED

In the fourth circle of Hell in Dante's *Inferno*, those who spent their lives steeped in greed fight each other with large weights that they push with their chests. These weights are depicted as bags of money and the people yell at one another, 'Why do you hoard?' and 'Why do you waste?' So, among the clergymen and cardinals who Dante observes, there are two manifestations of greed at war with one another for an endless era: the avaricious versus the prodigal.

—

I remember moving around a lot as a child.

My father stayed in the same house, but when my parents divorced, my mother moved us from home to home.

I remember a lot of boxes that remained unpacked so that each time we moved, there would be less to pack. It became difficult to keep track of what was in those boxes that were never reopened. Did we even miss them? Did we not open them because we feared that we would find we *did* miss those things – things we were so comfortable living without?

Why didn't we just get rid of them?

Were there really that many?

My memory isn't good. I think I remember things, but maybe I use it all to justify my behaviour as an adult. I think I remember things, but maybe I'm just making excuses. I think I remember things, but maybe it's easier to just be psychoanalysed.

Either way, as an adult who has to move zip codes every year because of rent or school or increasingly gentrified neighbourhoods, I still have a habit of amassing boxes I never open from one home to the next. Why do I have so much stuff? And more importantly, why can't I let go?

What am I hoping to find?

What am I hoping to keep?

—

A boss once asked me what my biggest strength was and I told her it was my ability to compartmentalize. She had never heard someone refer to that as a good quality, but I explained that it worked for me, especially in my career. I liked to compartmentalize because it helped me focus. It helped me mind different projects at different speeds and change gears on a dime when needed. It made me good at the things that I needed to be good at, put away things that I didn't need, or at least hold them off for a time.

The thing about compartmentalizing is that eventually you must open the compartments you thought you had closed, the ones you had only taped shut.

They can't stay sealed forever.

–

In 2017, my family asked me to return home to California, amid my youngest brother's medical crisis. The ask came shortly after being notified that I was going to be laid off.

A strange thing happens to a family when one of its members dies young. I'm still trying to figure out what that is and how exactly it's changed my family, but I know that it looks like a hole in every one of us, in the shape of a little boy. I think the hole sometimes alters our memories; alters the way we think. I know it alters the way I've viewed the passage of time, but I think that its size and shape are enough to change us almost entirely on the inside, while leaving our outsides the same.

In the aftermath of my brother's death, my family recalls that my situation in New York was more dire than I remember it being and that their asking me to return home was a helping hand for my sake.

I cannot say with any amount of certainty who was correct.

All I know is that I left California in 2012 a certain way. And when I returned in 2017, I was more the prodigal son than the daughter my father remembered, or the sister my brother may have only known.

–

If I could be greedy about one thing, it would be time. I would hoard it. As much of it as I can; so much that I could use it to go back.

And I would do my life all over again. Not as she or her, not as he or him, but as the sibling my brother never had a chance to really know. My identity was not something I discussed with him – the ten-year-old who passed away in 2017. When he saw me last, I was not yet transitioned. I had started on testosterone and was 45 lbs heavier than before, but he still called me his sister.

And forever, until I die, he'll have only called me his sister.

–

IV. Wrath

My father has a temper – he can get angry in a snap. As a teenager my mother would reprimand me, 'Are you going to be one of those angry lesbians?' Online, I see people writing about being targeted by 'those angry transgender people' for asking ignorant questions under the guise of innocent curiosity.

I feel responsible for representing all queer, trans, non-binary people all the time. We are so rare. Should I not be on my best behaviour, lest someone think ill of the community because of my actions?

My brother had a temper too. We would joke that he was just like our father, could fly off the handle, go from zero to a hundred in no time at all. Is it genetics, this quick anger? Do men who punch holes into their drywall just inherit the behaviour from their fathers and grandfathers?

I feel obligated to be the best version of a trans person I can possibly be. Because what if someone mistakes me for someone angry? For someone mad? For someone who hates allies and curious people with prying questions who are just trying to understand. Someone could see me punch a hole into drywall and think that I am the pinnacle of trans behaviour.

I can't be angry. I can't at all. What is there for me to be angry about? Me with all my privileges, my support, my medical access, my financial security. How can I be angry? Me, someone who has had access to everything I could possibly want?

How indeed?

—

V. ENVY

I have always been confused about the difference between envy and greed. I thought of them as so similar, it was hard to untangle one from the other. I used to think they were both about wanting material items. I've come to learn that envy is much more. Envy is wanting what somebody else already owns, what somebody else already has.

It is the deep, carnal desire to wear someone's skin so that you might experience the shiny, glossy view of the life you think they live.

—

A weird, sad thing happened to me as a teenager. It was so long ago, it feels as if it happened to somebody else. Perhaps it did, if we think of my personhood as split between before transition and after. Or else, it did because the people we are from one day to the next are constantly changing.

I feel silly admitting that the first relationship I was in, nearly half my life ago, still feels packed away in my subconscious, something I compartmentalized so I wouldn't have to examine it too closely. It's not that I'm ashamed that it happened, but that I'm ashamed that I might still use the effects of it to excuse some of my behaviour. But these were formative years of my life; maybe I should be more forgiving of myself. I should forgive the fact that these effects left scars that I can still graze over with my fingertips if I try.

This person that I embarked on my first relationship with was my best friend, which I feel is a common trope for young, queer people. We want to feel safe, loved, invincible. Who else can provide that but our friends? And who would experiment with us but those of our friends we called the best? Queer teenagers face the adversity of isolation, feeling as if we are the only ones to ever feel this brand-new feeling. As young queers we are alone until we find the one person wild enough and brave enough to take on the world side by side. It only makes sense that this person is usually our best friend.

I was sixteen. I was young and weird and queer, and in the conservative pocket of Irvine, California, I felt like I was the only person who knew that they were not straight. Until I met my best friend. And then it was us against the entirety of Irvine High School – our whole world.

I think of this person fondly, all these years later. The distance of time has made me forget hurt – no – has transformed that hurt into healing, and that healing into growth. But at the time it did not feel like growing.

It felt like being maimed at the root.

We fizzled out in the summer but with the fall came a new

school year, and the closeness of being in the same friend group, of attending the same classes, reawakened the carnal desires of our teenage hormones so that we found ourselves in bed together again, despite the fact that we remained apart. Then again. And again. And again. That big house, the twin-sized bed, the touching. After I was dumped, I didn't care what our public status was so long as I could touch this person again, love them again, be inside them again.

But that person never kissed me again after that summer, after we 'ended' our relationship. There was no romance or love there. I did the touching, but was never touched. And I'm not even sure that I was seen, really, because once when we were young and together in bed the name that escaped this person's mouth was not my name, but the name of a mutual friend.

I have tried to replay my teenage misadventures, to cut them and rearrange them so that I might better understand what happened. Even after all these years, all I come up with is that I envied a person I could not be, the person whose name slipped past the lips of someone I desperately tried to make love me. That was before I understood that that was not something you could make people do. I wanted what he had, which was something he didn't even know he possessed. I wanted to be him. I wanted to slip into his life, so I could wear his skin and be seen, and loved, and touched the way he did not know he could have been.

I envied him, our mutual friend, because I did not know that I could be loved as myself.

—

I want privilege.

That is what I envy, what I want from other people, the thing that other people possess that I do not have. I wonder what it must be like to walk around with the air of confidence that a particular kind of middle-class, cis, straight, able-bodied, white, millennial man possesses. I wonder what it must be like to be born and to be taught that nothing is above you and that the world is a series of steps you can just climb and climb and climb.

I want to take that privilege like a tangible object, something I could curl my fingers around and grasp in my palm so that I might clutch onto it tightly.

But I've had some privileges. I've had things that others would kill to take from me, just so they can step into my skin and see the end of the tunnel of transition, to see what it must be like to live in a body that is recognized in society as what its inhabitant wants to reclaim and represent. I want privilege, more of it, but I would share it if I could.

I see them, the people who struggle for the access I had, the people who do not know that they can be loved as themselves because we live in a society where the proclamation of identity is not performative enough to be validated by a discerning audience. I see them, and I've been them. And it has taken so much to get here, in small steps and giant leaps, but I would not go back to how it was before.

—

VI. SLOTH

If the seven deadly sins are by-products of too much want, then what is sloth an excess of? By its Latin definition, sloth is characterized by a complete and total lack. It is listlessness. It is uncaring. It is unmoving and lazy. In Dante's *Divine Comedy*, the punishment for sloth is found in the rings of *Purgatorio*, in the fourth circle where they (those who lived a slothful life) run endlessly in a circle. It's not Hell and it's not *Paradiso*, but it is punishment – and punishment for what? These were souls who failed to act in life for the pursuit of love, Virgil tells Dante. Sloth is not too much, the way lust and greed and gluttony are too much wanting, but a life lived without.

Finally, punishment for being empty.

It was one thing to fear eternal damnation for being too much. In sloth, you can feel like not enough.

–

Fundamentally, I disagree with the thought that sloth is a deadly sin, or even a sin at all. Perhaps because I have had depressive episodes in my life, I feel strongly that one person's idea of sloth is another person's reaction to a traumatic event.

I've never been formally diagnosed with depression so I maintain that I've never actually had it. 'Had it' though, makes it sound like a contagious disease. And maybe it is, sometimes, in that others can infect you with it, when they die. Or when they stop loving you.

I say that I've never had it, not because I would be ashamed to say that I have, but because I think that there's a very real distinction between being diagnosed with depression and just saying you're depressed. But depression impacts a large percentage of the population, especially in the United States, and especially when people are members of communities more marginalized than others. I don't feel ashamed to say that I probably could have been diagnosed with depression at some point (or points) in my life, but the truth of the matter is that I've eluded that diagnosis entirely.

My life took a turn in 2017. After my brother died, and while I was still living at home, I had lost all sense of direction. I had left my job, did not know what I wanted to pursue, and lived in a place where I could not afford rent on my own. I felt stuck in my parents' home. The only goals I did have were my goals of transition. When I moved back to California, I was extremely lucky to be able to go on Medi-Cal because of my unemployment status, and because I was on Medi-Cal, my top surgery would be covered through California's health care system. This $8,000 procedure that I had wanted my whole life was suddenly within my reach and the only thing I could do was to go on a waitlist. It was the only goal I could stick to, the only direction in which I felt myself pulled.

What my family probably saw was somebody who had suffered the same terrible tragedy that they had suffered, but who was not doing much to move past it. I know that it's hard to see yourself with any amount of clarity, but they were not in the room with me during my therapy sessions. They were not with me when I did the work of unpacking those mental boxes that I had moved from place to place. They were not with me when I was entrenched in dysphoria and a deep, unfathomable sadness. What they saw was someone who looked as if they were just waiting: waiting without direction, without follow-through, without care. A listless life without the pursuit of love.

The thought of accomplishing just one transition goal was enough to keep me going, keep me getting up every day so that I could have one single thing to look forward to. I had no idea if it would change my life for the better. Any modicum of improvement in my life, after my brother died, seemed impossible.

Every single day between my brother's death and my surgery, I felt that it was unbearable to generate any kind of joy for my future. Moving on seemed so daunting – at times it felt like betrayal. How could I leave my beloved brother behind? I loved him, didn't I? Then how could I do that to him? How could I change? How could I even think about a future without him if I loved him so much?

There's no social clout gained in claiming sloth as your sin the way there is for wrath or lust or even envy. We do not gain anything for being without direction, for living without the pursuit of love. Maybe that's why the punishment for sloth is not in Hell but in Purgatory. Maybe only the devil has sympathy for a life lived listlessly, aimless and without direction. Though I have never been formally diagnosed with depression, I think I understand being on the brink of it. Why would I have wanted to do anything if it meant that time alone took me away from my brother?

I had to move on. I knew this. I needed to do it at my own pace, as slowly as possible, or else I would have felt like I was leaving him behind too quickly. I did not resist healing because I desired to live a life without the pursuit of love. I resisted healing because I cared so much for somebody who was no longer here that the thought of going on without him was almost enough to kill me.

–

VII. Pride

Pride is the root of all sin – the genesis of all other sins – committed because humanity wanted to be closer to God. In *Inferno*, Satan is frozen in ice at the centre of Hell, punished for his audacity to rebel against God. In the Bible, Eve's pride compels her to take a bite of the apple in the Garden of Eden – the devil tempts her with the promise that if she eats the apple, she will 'be like God', know good and evil as God does, gain God's knowledge.

To be prideful, then, is to see oneself as being close to a state of godliness.

And if I should be punished for that? Then punish me.

–

June is Pride Month in the United States. It started with Pride marches after the Stonewall riots, which many people consider to be the start of the civil rights movement for LGBTQ+ communities. Those marches became weeklong events. Now the entire month of June is celebrated as an occasion to learn about, appreciate and pay homage to the history of LGBTQ+ people.

The first Pride parade I went to was in San Francisco. I can't remember what year it was, whether or not I had started college already or if I was a senior in high school. Was I out? I don't remember. I must have been if I was at a Pride parade in one of my favourite cities . . . but my memory . . . I don't remember the parade route. I can't recall who the grand marshal was that year or even who I was with. But I remember the exuberance of it, the kinetic, almost feverish atmosphere. It was not quite joy and it was not quite fear either. I know that it was at a tumultuous time for the community in California, right around Proposition 8, when they put gay marriage to a vote on California ballots. Thinking back, it reminds me of water pushing up against a dam. Something ready to burst.

Though I don't remember the granular details of that day, I remember Dykes on Bikes at my first Pride parade with complete clarity.

In 1976, Dykes on Bikes, a chartered lesbian motorcycle club, first headed the San Francisco Pride parade. From what I gather, they've been a part of it ever since. Before my first parade, I didn't think they were real. Even though I grew up in a progressive city, I didn't know anything about the LGBTQ+ community. I barely knew about the L and the G and gave in to harmful, stereotypical jokes about the B.

I did not know about slurs. I did not know about words like dysphoria and how it applied to me. I did not know about the many varied textures of the community and its broad spectrum of diversity. I couldn't have told you what heteronormativity was, let alone how one could be enacting within its parameters in compulsory ways. I had no idea about intersectionality, about the history of the word 'queer' and why I would fight to identify as it; I didn't even know what place the Asian-American community had in the LGBTQ+ community, if any.

So you can imagine my surprise at the majestic (and very real) appearance of Dykes on Bikes. As a budding queer, I saw these women as a picture of everything I'd been told not to be. They were beautiful and strong and tough – a picture of masculinity and butch confidence that I'd never known to exist before. With their leather jackets and weathered faces, they were a beacon I suddenly found myself looking toward. I never knew that kind of self-esteem, that kind of joy in fully being in one's own skin, could exist and ooze out of a person.

Their confidence seemed so easy, so natural, that I probably thought that they were always that way. How could I have imagined that those same women, whose motorcycle engines echoed around Embarcadero, had once felt an iota of insecurity or doubt? It seemed improbable to me that they had ever questioned their identity or were ever ashamed of the people I saw them as.

That was years ago, and I still remember them. I don't know any of them but I know that I love them. I love the roar of their motorcycles and the look of their sun-worn leather jackets. I love the way they wait to start the parade they've headed since before I knew what Pride was.

Their visibility, their confidence, their pride – I thought they were as close to godliness as I could get.

–

I read once that life expectancy for transgender people was thirty-four years. That thought never went away and after the forty-fifth president and his particular administration, I have to wonder – will it happen to me? Will I be the target of hate-based violence? The closer I creep towards thirty-four years young, the more I think about it. I dream of celebrating my thirty-fifth birthday with all the planning and grandeur of a wedding, because I want to be able to say that I made it: that I was allowed to grow old.

I think about all the times I did not want to grow old. I think about sloth, the depression, the void of emotion that could only be perceived as 'without care'. I think about envy – how I wanted to crawl out of my own being and become somebody else fully and completely. I think about wrath and all the times I never knew that I could be angry just to be angry. I think about greed and all my unpacked boxes, the towers of them in the warehouse of my soul that I sometimes hoped would open all at once, just to suffocate me. I think about gluttony, the want for food, consuming just to consume, being just to be, wondering if it was easier to go back to pretending that I was okay with what I was born with. I think about lust.

I think about all the times I did not want to grow old and know that I kept going anyway.

I get to write this down for you because I kept going. Christianity will tell anybody that the seven deadly sins are a path toward eternal damnation, but I can't help but think it was those sins that saved me. It was all of it: the lust for wanting so desperately to be loved; the gluttony for eating well so that I could keep going; the greed for all the time I want to hoard so that someday I would have so many stories to tell my brother; the wrath to keep raging against the world that says that I have a life expectancy of thirty-four years; the sloth that only looked like listlessness because nobody could feel what I felt.

And pride.

—

I was in New York City the day Andrew Cuomo signed the Marriage Equality Act, that Friday before Pride weekend in 2011.

I was twenty-one and it was the summer between my junior and senior years in college. I'd been grappling with some self-esteem issues over the course of my third year and I needed New York City to give me a new perspective on life, otherwise I wasn't sure what I would do if I kept going on that way.

It was the summer I finally cut off all my hair, something that I'd wanted to do for a while. I polled friends. Some people thought I could pull off the look and some people were apprehensive. But I cut my hair many summers ago and I've never grown it out since.

This was also the summer that I started to identify as a lesbian instead of bisexual. It was the summer of change and wonderment. My world expanded a hundred-fold all because I went on that summer trip to New York City to visit my best friend. I didn't do the Pride parade that year – no, I attended the Dyke March, which takes place on a Saturday (while Pride takes place on Sunday – Sundays are important and holy after all). The Dyke March is different. On its website, the organization emphasizes that it is not a parade; it is a protest. There's a different kind of energy to the Dyke March than there is to the Pride parade – it's something fierce and bold, something angry, something that comes only when the reclamation of self is totally realized. Dykes on Bikes have that energy; the Dyke March has that energy.

I wanted that energy so badly. I wanted to know what it felt like to wield the power of an identity that can only be described as a reclamation from an oppressive majority. I did not know how I would get there. I could not see the path toward confidence, and I could not align myself with these people who seemed to live a life so free, I couldn't imagine that we had anything in common.

I might not have reclaimed the title of dyke for myself, but I did find that energy for my own reclamation of identity. It started there, with the breeze blowing through my newly cut hair. And it started before that, too – as if the roar of the engines from Dykes on Bikes began to awaken me. These women were a part of my future in ways that I wasn't able to fully comprehend, in ways that I am still learning about. It started in those summers, in the month of June – during Pride.

I wanted to be like them, these women, these people who lived lives that seemed so free and out. It was like nothing could touch them. Intellectually, I know this to not be true. I know that they were probably people who rode the subway home afterward and scrubbed off the layers and various colours of body paint, who tried to make sure they washed the glitter down the drain before work the next day. But to me, and quite possibly to themselves, during those days of protests and those marches of pride, they seemed untouchable, invincible and beautiful beyond measure.

–

June 2019, the fiftieth anniversary of the Stonewall riots.

On 28 June 1969, police spontaneously raided the Stonewall Inn, a gay bar in New York's West Village. When the raid happened, fights broke out – people had had enough. Whenever I've learned about the Stonewall riots, I've heard two names: Marsha P. Johnson, a black transwoman, and Stormé DeLarverie, a butch lesbian. Their legacies are integral to the gay liberation movement of the late sixties and seventies.

But that's who started it – LGBTQ+ pride. That's where it started: with the L and the T. With wrath. With having enough. And with the pride to stand up and fight back.

At the time of writing, my partner is in the living room, sprawled across the couch, reading a book she'll finish by tonight and want me to read right after so that we can talk about it together. Our cat is curled up on the other end, asleep like he always is. We live in Los Angeles, where the summer is burning hot and our air conditioner is always running. We live in an area with a large, young, gay population. On a clear day, we can see the Hollywood sign from our front door.

Before I go to sleep tonight, I'll ask my partner to turn the lights down and I will kiss her as if I haven't kissed her all day. I usually do the cooking because hers doesn't extend to foods typically eaten after noon, so tomorrow she'll make breakfast because I've asked and because I love the way she makes oatmeal (which is to say that she adds a lot of peanut butter). We unpacked our last box today, but I still have a lot of photos to hang – partly pictures of our shared trips but mostly snapshots of my brother, who my partner never got to meet but wants to have in the house anyway. Not much makes me angry, other than the fact that we only have twenty-four hours in a day and when it comes down to it, there's nobody I would rather be because they don't get to live this life with her.

If I'm lucky, I can convince her to take a nap together, us and the cat on the couch with the air conditioning running.

I'm proud of this boring picture of domesticity.

I will never have that same energy those women from my formative past had. I know we share a community, that our stories are more similar than I thought at the time when I first saw them, but we don't have the same story. That's okay, because I learned from them.

I modelled my trans pride after them and though we are similar, it's true that we are also different. Dykes on Bikes and the Dyke March are reclamations of an identity that was previously a word used to oppress the other. I cannot call myself a dyke – I cannot reclaim that identity for part of myself. But their strength and pride showed me the way to my own identity. To my own pride.

To claim my transness is my pride.

To live as a trans person, in this body that I love and is loved by someone else, is my pride. To eat well and take care of myself is my pride. To be greedy about my time and the way I spend it remembering and forging ahead is my pride. To know I can be angry and to own that anger is my pride. To live lavishly in this world, to squander the unlimited well of my happiness, is my pride. To sometimes falter and ask for a break is my pride. I proudly live a perfectly boring, domestic, trans life.

Pride is the root of all sin. We act on pride because we dare to think that we can be closer to God, that we can become godlike.

Every day I keep going – a person who dared to be like God.

Snapshots for memory

A little boy looking down at the teddy bear he's holding. There is another person beside him, mostly out of frame, apart from one of his feet.

In a white frame with a white mat, between the front door and the large north-facing windows, there lives a photo. It's a photo of two of my brothers, the oldest and the youngest, but all you can see of the oldest is his foot, and perhaps, if you're squinting, the side of his face. Most of the photo is dark black, muddied, badly composed. But in the centre is my youngest brother, face tilted downward, smiling.

In the foreground is a scrap of wrapping paper from a present someone received that year. I remember what I got, only because it was used to capture this photo: a camera lens. I don't know if you would be able to tell that the photo was taken on Christmas Day. The discarded wrapping paper is inside-up, blank white belly pointed to the sky, but my brother's blue pyjamas have polar bears wearing red scarves on them. Maybe if you've been inundated with Coca-Cola commercials since you were a child, you would get that this was taken at Christmas.

But I can't unknow what I already know about this photo.

In this mostly dark photo of my brother and his polar bear pyjamas, the light is only illuminating his face and the thing he is holding. His face is full and round, the way children's faces are. His smile is delicate. It's the smile of someone unaware that they are being observed, the kind reserved for something or someone deeply loved. I look at that photo and I think that my lips sometimes tip upward into that kind of smile too – the kind reserved for someone deeply loved. Sometimes I go out to my north-facing windows, stand in the middle of the living room and stare at this photo. A break in my day.

The look on my brother's face, that look of care and love and kindness, is because of the thing he is holding, also gently lit in the photo. It is a brand-new stuffed animal, but not just any stuffed animal. This is a TY Pluffies My Baby Bear in brown, with soft sewn eyes. It can be found on eBay for about $50. I know this because my brother had about seven of them. Every year, for Christmas, Santa would come and place a brand-new version of this bear into my brother's stocking. And every year, my brother would love it.

Santa got me gifts too, left something small in my stocking. Santa kept visiting me throughout my teens and into my twenties, the benefit of being an oldest sibling. The gifts might have gotten smaller as time when on, but there was always something in my stocking, wherever it was hung. It was when my brother died that Santa stopped leaving me presents, stopped visiting completely.

When new people come by, maintenance workers, or new neighbours, they always comment on it because it is right by the front door.

'What a beautiful picture,' they say. 'Is that your . . . ?'

'Yep, that's my brother,' I say, answering the unasked question for them because I always see the math they do in their heads, the mental gymnastics, wondering if he is brother or son. And I say it as if he's still alive. Still receiving Christmas presents every year. Still holding those bears that he loves so much, smiling like he will get a new one if the old one falls apart.

Photographs are supposed to help us remember. They're meant to help us see things as they were, when they were. But sometimes, when somebody comes to my home and asks about the beautiful photo I have hung where it will be most visible, I tell a lie. I act as if the photo was taken recently, or 'last Christmas'. Sometimes I say that he's still ten even though he has been dead since 2017. Sometimes I say that this is an older photo, that he lives in the Bay Area with my parents. I pretend that, for a moment, he has a life outside of mine, somewhere just beyond me. That he is and not was.

I do that a lot with him, and not just when people ask about the photo. I like to think that he does have a life outside of mine, somewhere I cannot see. I think of him as growing and being and playing in some parallel universe or other dimension, just . . . somewhere. Somewhere else.

That somewhere must be great. Otherwise, why hasn't he tried to come back?

A poster, 3 ft by 4 ft, framed cheaply in glossy black wood, behind a plastic protector. An infant, in a bathtub, is sitting naked in a safety chair. The chair is blue with yellow accents. The infant is smiling, hair wet, toes splayed. The infant's ears are pierced.

How do I talk about my past?

I tread around my past in the same way other transgender and non-binary people do, I'm sure. We do not all tread with the same light-footedness, but I find myself leaning towards anecdotes of the more recent past.

'When I was a little girl . . .'

I use the statement sparingly. It works, sometimes, for the way I tell certain things about my childhood, depending on the company I'm keeping. I grew up socialized a certain way with the constraints of a certain gender and so, for my personal experience and life story, I don't completely sidestep the time when I was a little girl.

I think of my gender as an evolution of where I was to where I am today, which is not the experience of all transgender people. The gender I was assigned at birth is in my past, a gender that I will sometimes refer to as a part of me then but not a part of myself now. I still prefer genderless or gender-neutral framings of my childhood, but growing up with the expectations of an assigned gender has shaped the way I react to my world or have reacted to my world. Those expectations shaped the decisions I made about activities I wanted or could have participated in. Gender formed my friendships, steered me toward expected groups of people (mostly girls) while limiting close friendships with others (often boys). The gender I was expected to perform was a role I was required to play, with expectations I needed to fulfil, and a lens through which others viewed me. I danced around it as much as anyone else. We created a society that relied on gender to frame our lives.

Two things can be true at once: I identify as transgender and non-binary; there was a time when I was a little girl. This is how I approach my history as a trans person. But not all trans people approach their history in the same way.

This photo of baby me hung in the first house I remember, above my parents' bed, a long time ago when they were still together. I was my parents' first child. And because they had me when they were young, I was everyone else's first child too. An experiment, mostly, but I guess some people prefer to call children miracles. So that's what I was. The first miracle to family and friends, all young twenty-somethings in San Francisco in the early nineties. Acid-washed jeans, oversized sweaters, hair that defied gravity . . . and me.

Because I was the first and it was the nineties and film was more accessible than it had ever been before, there are a lot of photos of me. I had a big head that I think I grew into. I've never held these photos as we didn't take them with us when we moved away from my father's house. And he changed homes as well. So they were stored. Tucked away in the attic of my father's most recent home.

My sister makes my father take them down sometimes, which is how I know they exist. I have no memories associated with these snapshots, no recollection of posing or smiling. This poster could be of any infant. It could be anyone's favourite daughter. Or least favourite. Or middle child. It could be a neighbour or a cousin. It is a photo of a little girl whose facial features resemble mine. I only know it's me because I've been told.

Which is how I feel about these photos of a young me, these photos of me that exist without my consciousness of the moment – they may as well be of someone else. I don't feel much of anything when they're shown to me. Who is this happy, smiling child, not a care in the world, in the warm water of a bath and with a parent who is taking the photo?

My memories of growing up, between this photo of infant me and into my pre-teen years, are hazy. They're almost all like that, like memories of a badly remembered movie, disjointed scenes that don't encompass a whole plot. Maybe I don't want to remember the connecting narrative, the whole synopsis. Simply forgetting is easier than trying to dredge up an old me, a me that acted in a way that was expected of girls. How much of my childhood was mine and how much of it was what I thought I needed to do?

I don't know. I don't really want to know. I don't want to dig up the signs that I was trans and non-binary all along. It would hurt too much to really understand that I felt so different so early on in my life, but I never had the language or means of being myself.

This photo is a polaroid. A child with long hair is standing in the dining room, eyes sleepy, but smiling. They are wearing a dark child-sized suit and a nice white shirt.

Here is a memory I may actually have, one that is real, if only because I feel like I can validate it.

When I was five, I badly wanted a suit. Because I was the first child to young parents who had no concept of what an age-appropriate movie was, I had seen *Pulp Fiction*. It wasn't the violence or the drug use that left an impression on my malleable young mind. Instead, it unlocked a deep desire for me to obtain a suit.

As the story goes, nobody wanted to buy me one. There would be no occasion to wear it, it would be an extravagant waste of money, and also, it just seemed odd. Who buys a little girl a suit?

Worn down by begging or pouting, someone eventually bought me a suit.

And I wore it several times, mostly as a costume. Sometimes with a painted-on moustache to complement it and styled with suspenders even though the pants had a belt loop. There are several photos of me, with the jacket on and the jacket off, a smirk on my five-year-old face, trying desperately to channel John Travolta.

Eventually, I grew out of that suit, but I loathed dresses and skirts. As I grew older, I found myself gravitating towards the boys' and men's section of clothing stores, even for simple things like T-shirts and jeans, socks even. I preferred the boxier, baggier look that boys' clothes gave me over the flared jeans and capped-sleeved T-shirts that were in the girls' section. In girls' clothes I felt exposed. The tightness in the arms and hips made me uncomfortable. I gave in for special occasions, allowing my family to put me in a dress for tradition and appearances, but it always felt like an awkward costume that I couldn't wait to stop wearing.

I wouldn't get another suit until I was an adult. I wore them semi-regularly in an office setting and I started to enjoy the feeling suits gave me. They felt natural to be in and I liked the power and formality they lent me. I liked the different ways the same suit could be accessorized with a tie or a change of shoes. I felt validated when men complimented my sartorial choices and attention to detail, as if I was wearing their clothes better than they ever could.

I no longer have to pout to obtain a suit. I can put on one of the many in my closet whenever I please. This old polaroid isn't the only one that exists of me wearing a suit anymore and I'm no longer standing sleepily in dining rooms in an outfit that feels like a secret.

Three teenagers are standing by the drop-off circle in front of a swimming centre. Daylight reveals that it's morning. One of the teenagers is wearing dark blue jeans and a black T-shirt with an Iron Man graphic. They have an orange traffic cone on their head. Their two friends are laughing.

Where are the kids in this photo today?

I've lost touch with them. All of them, including the one that resembles me – the one who is causing all the laughter, traffic cone stolen from some parking space. That person feels very far away. I've distanced myself from this person on purpose. It feels painful to even think about being that person; there is an ache when I try to put myself back into this photo, my body physically rejecting the mental exercise. Remembering high school feels like grief. And though I have lived so much and so fully after those four brief years, I still have trouble putting into words why those memories feel like hurt.

In some ways it's delayed embarrassment. I think most people share that experience of remembering themselves at that age. I'm not just embarrassed about my taste in music and clothing but because I was trying so hard to be someone else, and I didn't even know it.

At the same time, that person feels alien to me. Imagine trying to have someone else's memories. That's how it feels to try to remember what it was like to be this person with those friends in that time – I can't quite do it. I'm not convinced that those memories are mine. That teenager was sad and weird and didn't have the language for why. Why grieve at such a young age? Why be so hurt by the world with so much life still left to live?

I have distanced myself from that teenager in the photo. I skip that part of my life, only relay it in vague anecdotes, try to be relatable through music trends and popular culture of the time. They are all surface level, the stories I tell from my teenage years.

So here is where something starts. The distancing. The severance. Every iteration of myself cuts a path from past to present, changes friends, changes cities, changes changes changes.

Until nothing is left but a photo.

A person with short hair is standing on a long paddle board, oar partially in the water. They are wearing sunglasses, a blue hoodie from US Rowing and red shorts. They are barefoot and tan.

The caption reads: 'So this is what I look like now.'

The summer between my junior and senior years in college, I cut off all my hair and started wearing contact lenses. Cropping my hair was something I wanted to do for a long time before I actually did it. And when I did finally go to get it cut, it was while I was visiting a friend in New York City. I found a random unisex salon and asked for it all to be taken off.

'Like a boy,' I said.

'Are you sure?'

I wasn't. At the time, I was still solidly and comfortably in my identity as a lesbian. And like many young, baby queers, I was butchphobic. Did I want to cut off all my hair? Did I really want to be *that butch*? The practical side of me said yes. I could never figure out what to do with my hair when it was long. Put it in a ponytail, let my sideswept bangs do what they will. Or, if it was for a party, straighten it with the heat of a hundred ovens. Fry it to hell and back and call it a night.

But there was a scared side of me too. As if cutting my hair was a commitment to a lifestyle and I wasn't quite sure what that lifestyle entailed or if I was ready to make that choice. How did I want to be perceived? It was a question I once didn't know I could ask or have any control over. Once I started asking it, I couldn't stop. How did I want to be perceived? What did I want to look like to others? I didn't yet have a complete answer, an answer that felt totally right.

I knew that the way I was perceived with long hair was not what I wanted. I didn't feel like it was a part of me that fit. When people saw my long hair, they assumed things about me. Gendered things. And knowing that made me feel uncomfortable. It made me feel like I stuck out in people's minds as wrong, like they could tell I didn't like my long hair. They could tell the way I presented didn't match the way I wanted to present.

I cut it all off, flew back to California, hung out with some friends at Newport Beach, then posted this photo of myself on Facebook before the school year started. The comments were positive. I was relieved and then I went on with my life with this new look, a look that I think is very natural. It's the other photos, the photos with the long hair that feel truly alien. The photos of me with short hair in college still seem far away, but they are not nearly as distant as the photos of me in high school.

My hair grows and grows, and it wasn't long before I discovered that I would have to get many more haircuts to maintain a short cut than I ever did with long hair. And though I hated it when my hair got too long and started to tickle the backs of my ears, for a long time going to a barbershop was hard. Which was probably what resulted in my man-bun phase. But I digress.

It took a long time to find a barber with whom I felt comfortable.

Andrew was my first regular barber after my top surgery. He cut my hair while I was in Ireland and, no offence to my current barber, he gave me some of my best haircuts. He would chat with me about his family, tell me about the vacations he wanted to take with his wife and kids, and always remembered the kind of haircut I liked. He was professional and courteous. He thought my name was James, which was the name I always gave when I made an appointment. He asked me about school and how my courses were going and when I mentioned that I was getting a haircut because my girlfriend was coming to visit, he asked me about the visit the next time he saw me. That was his barbershop talk. Just normal banter.

I thought about Andrew when I returned to the States and was in desperate need of a cut. I thought about how easy it was to just book with Andrew, how I didn't worry about stepping into his shop. I thought about the old anxieties of walking into male-dominated spaces, fearing that I wouldn't pass and they would make fun of me or ruin my hair or refuse me service. I made the mistake of booking an appointment through Yelp, under the name Jayne. I will never forget what that barber said to me while I was sitting in the chair, razor buzzing by my ear, his hands flitting against my scalp.

'What kind of name is Jayne? Your dad not around to stop your mom from giving you that name?'

Barbershop talk is a strange world for me to navigate. I admit to leaning into misogyny and cracking 'happy wife, happy life' jokes because it seems safer than not agreeing or keeping quiet, but this comment felt . . . different. Barbershop talk is usually vague generalizations about men and masculinity. It's usually ribbing one another for having 'overbearing spouses' or 'being a bum' or what have you. The usual banter never sounds like anything personal, except that this did.

It's one thing to question someone's given name, but to follow it up with the assumption that my dad wasn't around and that's why I have 'a girl's name' is something else. Something gross. Something deeper than preconceived notions about how people should be or act. There is fault in my name and the fault must clearly be the lack of a proper masculine presence. I made up something stupid, said it was a family name, and then he told me about the shirt-making business that was going to make him a lot of money. I never went back there.

Eventually, a friend introduced me to my current barber. Fausto doesn't ask too many questions, which I like, because he doesn't pressure me into being something that I feel uncomfortable being. He always has great music recommendations and the banter between him and the rest of the barbers feels a lot less centred around overly masculine topics. Like Andrew, Fausto is professional, courteous and always remembers small things about me. I go to Fausto because he gives me a good haircut, but also because he doesn't ask anything else of me.

Nowadays, most people assume that I have been going to barbershops my whole life, that I grew up going with my dad to get his hair cut and that I just know what a 2 or a low fade or a hard part is. They don't know that I ever frantically made things up or agreed to numbers I didn't know the meaning of as I tried to find a barber who wouldn't make me look like a joke.

So I look like this now, and they think that I always have.

A person sitting up in a hospital bed throws up a peace sign with their fingers, though they are frowning. They have an IV in their wrist and their hospital tag is visible. They are holding a paper cup with two popsicle sticks in it. There is still some red popsicle on one of them.

The caption reads, 'I lived, bitch.'

I had eaten four red popsicles by the time I left UCSF's hospital and my friend Celina drove me back home. She's the one who took the photo. I look tired, beyond tired – I look exhausted.

This was seven months after my brother died, six days after sleeping with my partner for the first time, and fifty-three days before I would move to Ireland. Life was moving fast, I had just gotten out of a major surgery, so of course I look exhausted. But still. Maybe I should have cracked a smile.

I was loved here in this photo, with Celina taking it and my partner sending text messages to me in my bleary, post-anaesthesia state. I look so miserable, but I know, in hindsight, that I was loved. That Celina loved me enough to pick me up and take me to my surgery. That my partner loved me enough to begin a relationship with me during such a tumultuous time.

I had started to accumulate things to look forward to because I was afraid of what depression was doing to me. I had pressed on with my appointments for my top surgery. I had put down a deposit to attend school in Ireland. I had turned a casual relationship into a long-term one. I had found reasons to keep going, one day at a time, from the first red popsicle to today. Some days I'm still not sure why. But I keep going. Perhaps for love.

Images are supposed to be proof that we were here, that we looked like that, that we did that thing in that moment, but photographs show only what is there in the frame. So much of our lives happen out of frame, out of sight. There was a brief period of time after my top surgery but before I got my right arm tattoos, of which there is no photographic proof. I asked friends if they had photos but nobody could conjure up my bare arm and breastless torso in the same digital frame.

Photographs are supposed to be memories, but I have forgotten so much. So many photographs evoke pain just by looking at them. They make me feel like I changed too much, lost too much, let go of too much. They make me feel guilty for being happy and different now. They make me feel guilty for being happy and different then.

You can't photograph love. Not really. You can photograph smiles and moments, things that are there. But you can't photograph the enormity of love, no matter how much you could wax poetic about a photograph. How can you prove that love exists in the frame? All that love that happened between one photo and the next, all the love that surrounded this tired person sitting in a hospital bed – that can't be captured inside a single image.

A child is smiling, maybe laughing, facing the camera. They have a nasal cannula wrapped around their face. The black straps of an oxygen backpack are on their shoulders, over a nice collared shirt.

After Ireland, I came back to California to live with my partner. She lets me put up photographs all around the house, photos from my travels, of our friends, of my family. We even hang photos of us, though they are all comically bad. We have art, from reproductions of bright, abstract, silhouettes or women rowing and pastoral seaside villas to hand-drawn, original pieces by my sister. I have grandiose dreams of hanging a gallery wall from floor to ceiling by our staircase.

I hang photos to remind me of smiles, frowns and traffic cones. I hang mundane photos and silly candids, professional wedding photography and Instax prints.

I hang photos of my brother in as many places as I can. One of his school photos is stuck to the fridge with a magnet. On picture day, he would always be reminded to take his oxygen tank off, so in many of his school photos his nasal cannula and backpack straps are missing. In one of his later photos, the cannula is still there, his smile that's crossed with a laugh forever in frame with his oxygen tubes. You might think the photographer did a great job of capturing that smile, but it's more likely that my brother told a joke and, in telling his joke, made himself laugh, and so the photographer only had to press a button, laughing along too.

Photos of my brother show that he was. That he was here with us and that he made us laugh and made himself laugh too. They might show his cannula or his oxygen tank, but they do not show his tenacity or stubbornness. They do not show how he cheated at card games or got mad and cried when he lost. They show only that he was here. A boy.

As I age and move further away from the smiling infant in a tub and the teenage friends in the parking lot and the two popsicles in a paper cup, I am also moving away from a boy with his oxygen backpack in his school photo. A memory. No new photos of a boy who cannot be photographed. But that does not mean no new memories. No, every time I tell a story of my brother, I create a new snapshot in my mind with him. And though he is not there to make me laugh or shed tears, I capture the moment when I'm telling you about him, and I make a new memory to keep him here with me.

With my brother's photos displayed around our house and people coming and going in our lives, I wonder if we will ever reach a time when someone catches a glimpse of him along our stairwell and asks if that was me as a child. Don't we look related?

I will tell them no, that's not me as a child, and then I will create a new memory.

Better, sweeter

My partner and I haven't been together for very long, although we've known each other since 2011. We only really started becoming *a thing* six days before I was scheduled to have my bilateral mastectomy. With all the love and care I thought only existed between two people who had been together for a long while, she made me a number of portioned, low-sodium meals to eat after my surgery. She gave them to me sheepishly.

'I'm not sure how good they'll taste,' she said. 'They're a little bland without salt.'

—

My brother, only ten years old, died in November 2017. That was eight months before my surgery. Our family seemed to implode with such force that it exploded too – the big bang. The death of my brother was the birth of an alternate universe for us: one in which he did not exist. We lived in parallel realities from our timeline when he was with us to the timeline when he was not.

Sometimes, I think that I was the only person who knew he was going to die.

He'd been sick since he was born, an extremely premature

birth at twenty-two weeks and five days gestation. At ten years old, he needed a lung transplant to keep going. Half of all patients who receive a lung transplant don't make it a full year. He had only one working lung when he was placed on the list. Everything seemed against him. But what kind of people would my family be if they were not optimistic about his health?

At times, I felt like I was a monster for thinking that he was not going to make it, that he would not get the transplant. Or worse, that he would and he would simply die on the table. I stopped myself short of thinking of the borrowed time that we could manage to get out of someone else's lung. My brother, whom I loved so ardently, was never old in my imaginings. I had never allowed myself to see him as an adult, as a teenager graduating from high school, as anything but that ten-year-old boy with the crooked teeth.

I loved him – still do – and never let myself think of what he would look like if he had gone through puberty.

–

Taking testosterone made me ravenous.

I ate everything I could. Every free dessert, snack, or meal offered by my place of work seemed to find its way into my hands, into my mouth. I had the appetite of a teenage boy but without the metabolism of one.

I never knew what contributed most to my weight gain: the testosterone or my depression. I was set to leave New York, to move back home to California to help my family while my brother relocated to Texas to wait for his lung transplant. I think I knew even then. I think I halted my thoughts as I readied to move out and return to the West Coast.

My body changed, grew, rounded as I packed up my things, figured out the logistics of my going. My shirts wouldn't fit and my feet grew a whole size. Even the ring I always wore became too tight.

Many of my physical changes were expected, the mildly anticipated side effects of taking testosterone. There were emotional alterations, too, though I can't say for certain whether it was the testosterone or the move that caused my mood swings and my brain chemistry to alter ever so slightly. What led me down, dragged me quietly and eerily into the place where I felt my real self slept?

I found it increasingly difficult to express joy. There were sincere thoughts behind the words that came out of my mouth, but something about my delivery was flat, deadened. I told people I would miss them, but it felt like I was dying instead of going away. And then, suddenly, there would be white hot flashes of anger about my situation, my brother's life, the unfairness of health. Just as suddenly, it would all flatline again.

—

My brother was a normal boy except for the fact that he always had a nasal cannula and a tank of oxygen with him. When he was younger, he had a few fine-motor-skill problems, but as he got older those went away. He played piano and ukulele, though he fought when he was told it was time to practice. He would have preferred to play on a screen. A normal boy.

A food therapist used to come to work with him. Not normal for a normal boy, I guess. It was normal for us – this man coming to teach my brother to eat and swallow. He showed up and chatted, became friends with our family. The night before we flew out to Texas, he came to pick up our dog which he would care for while we were away.

My brother had chewing exercises. He tended to keep things in his mouth without swallowing them. We thought it was partly psychological. He was, after all, adept at eating things like ice cream and candy without being reminded of having to swallow or chew properly. He liked sweets, that was about it. The pickiest eater in our whole family.

When it got really bad, when he needed calories, we would pump caloric-heavy formula into his gastronomy tube. When he got older, we would try to get him to drink it, but he hated the way it tasted. I couldn't blame him, to be fair. I tried it once. It didn't taste great. Sometimes we would have to give him some of his formula while he was asleep, through the G-tube. He would never wake up during this process, and I still have an alarm in my phone telling me to feed my brother his formula.

I don't know what his last meal was. I'm not sure any of us do. I feel like it would be weird and disrespectful if I were to ask about it now. But I wonder, sometimes, if it was the formula he hated so much, or something better – something sweeter.

When we arrived at Texas Children's Hospital, he was intubated. I believe the last words I said to my brother were on a FaceTime while he was still conscious.

'I love you! I miss you!'

And then the infection got worse and off we went, the rest of our family, to Houston to watch my brother cleave our lives in two: with him and without him.

I don't remember the last words I said to my brother, while he was unconscious, when they removed his breathing tube. They might have been the same; they must have been the same. But I wish they had been something better, something sweeter.

—

They said it took me a while to wake up after the anaesthesia wore off. I had a tube down my throat for four hours, maybe more. The nurse handed me a popsicle. It turned my tongue bright red.

She told me as soon as I was done with one popsicle, she could get me another. I ate four by the time I was able to dress myself in the bathroom and they helped me to the front of the hospital in a wheelchair. My friend who drove me to the hospital then drove me back to my parents' house. I fell asleep halfway through, lulled by painkillers.

My partner says she's disappointed she wasn't there for me when I had my surgery. She had planned a family trip to the East Coast before we got together. Even though we hadn't been together long, I think she loved me then, because I knew I loved her then. It's difficult for us to explain to our friends how we got from Point A to Point B. We both feel like our story is longer and richer than it really is.

After my brother died, it was difficult to find joy and meaning in anything in my life. I went to therapy every other week to try and make sense of living. I had problems at home that I find difficult to put into words, not because the wound is fresh but because I feel as though I cannot blame my family for the ways that we treated each other. It was worse than being feral, than lashing out at one another. We were like black holes, each one of us, sucking the light out of everything, growing dense with sorrow.

The lowest I had ever thought I would be – that's when my partner let me in.

I ate the low-sodium meals my partner prepared to keep the swelling down and texted her every morning, giving her updates on my aches and pains, showing her pictures of my bruising. She came back from the East Coast a week into my recovery, thirteen days after we first started to become *a thing*.

Beautiful and shy, she lay next to me, careful of my post-surgery drains and still-sore torso. Did I think about how I could finally lie next to her in a body that more closely resembled how I felt? I don't know. All I know is that she lay next to me and then we gave ourselves to each other, against doctor's orders. I wasn't allowed to have sex so close to having had a major surgery. I want to say something stupid like it felt like having sex for the very first time. But it was not that. It felt right. Right in a way that I don't have words for. Right in a way that I don't think many people have words for, when they experience a life-affirming surgery and then lie next to someone they think they might be falling in love with.

I missed her while she was away with her family, even though it was only for a short while. I needed her, in a way. It wasn't dependency, except maybe it was. I depended on that feeling she gave me, the feeling that life was going to keep moving on. She did not *save my life* the way people might want to romanticize it. What she gave me was something as close to living as I had felt since my brother had died. Something more than just surviving.

Something better.

Something sweeter.

—

My partner and my brother never met.

They will never meet.

They are two tines in the split fork of my life, running parallel to each other. I imagine them as physical embodiments of the alternate universe I felt crack and splinter off when my brother died. One is where he was, the other is where she will be.

It's difficult to think that two people who mean so much to me can never look one another in the eye. I have to tell her what he was like, recounting stories of him through the laughter of reminiscing. But I can't tell him about her. I can tell her about the funny things he said or did, but I can't tell him about how I think she's the smartest woman I've had a conversation with. That I find it endearing when she admits she doesn't understand a pop culture reference. That I love her even though she leaves the refrigerator open while she rummages about in the kitchen.

I don't think my partner and my brother were ever supposed to meet.

It's easier to think that this is how it's supposed to be than to give myself permission to imagine an alternate timeline where they are in the same room, laughing. Even if I did give myself permission to imagine it, it's hard to know where to begin. How would our relationship have happened without the unfortunate circumstances that brought us close to one another?

I was able to receive top surgery because I came to California to help my family as my full-time job. Without that, I would not have been able to get onto Medi-Cal, the medical insurance that covered the cost of my double mastectomy, something that I was nowhere near able to afford before I had that coverage. Had my brother not died, I wouldn't have found a therapist who was able to connect me within my network to my surgeon, on top of working with me on my mental health. Had I not had my surgery and that access to therapy, would I have truly known the beginnings of a blossoming love between myself and my partner?

It's hard to say.

Karen Blixen once wrote that 'The cure for anything is salt water: sweat, tears or the sea.' I think about all the salt in my life. The tears and the sweat, the Pacific Ocean, which I grew up so close to, as well as the Atlantic. I think about all the times I could not cry when I first started testosterone, an effect I'd been warned about. I think about all the tears after my sweet brother passed on. I think about the sweat I poured trying to tune my body toward something as true to my sense of self as I could get. I think of the fact that my brother and my partner have never met, can never meet. What could possibly cure all that hurt?

And then I think of my partner, who handed me a batch of meals and said, 'They're a little bland without salt.' I think of the way she asks me to tell her something else about my brother. I think of the way her eyes well up with tears when she listens, or the way she laughs with me as I talk. I think of the way she asks about the scene, like she's recreating it in her mind.

I think, *Is the cure for everything truly salt water?*
Or is it something better, something sweeter?

AND FINALLY

I have a habit that my wife thinks is awful.

I will read the first twenty or so pages of a new book and then skip to the end and read the very last page. There are a few conditions, though. I only do this with novels, never with short stories or essays. If the last page is only a few lines, I don't cheat and read the page before it. If there is an epilogue, I read the last page before the epilogue.

I've done it for as long as I can remember, always thumbing back to the last page. Ninety-nine times out of a hundred, the last page doesn't contain spoilers. Sometimes there is an unfamiliar name. Sometimes there is dialogue that makes little sense. But more often than not, the author has found a way to capture finality in atmosphere alone. Whether it's characters staring off into the distance or looking back at where they came from, standing alone in an empty room or getting lost in a crowd – even if the book has a planned sequel, so much of the last page is just . . . the feeling of an ending. Finality.

I have made up reasons for doing this as the years roll on. When I am feeling intellectual, I make sweeping statements about doing it because of craft. I might say that I want to see where authors intend to get before I have gotten there. But really,

I just like to peek. The occasional spoiler isn't always what the plot hinges on. Sometimes someone is dead or is dying and that's always jarring. But that's also life, in a way.

We cannot skip to the last pages of each interaction we have with another person. We can't find our endings before we are ready for them or they for us.

So maybe that's another reason I do it. Just to know that some things end, neatly and plainly, with the flip of a page.

—

After my brother, I left for Dublin and then Los Angeles, where I have lived since. I have not been back to visit my parents. Not for holidays nor for a visit. I hear that my brother's ashes are still in a box, wrapped in that nondescript green velvet bag.

When I think of my parents, I try to think of a time when they loved me. I know that they loved me in their own way, but it's difficult to find warmth or affection in my memories of them. What I remember most are the ways in which we lost ourselves after we lost my brother. We became different people after he died because parts of us went with him. And sometimes I think that the parts we lost were the best parts of us. We can never go back to the people we were before. We can never become the family we had been.

I have tried my best to understand the grief that my parents went through. I understand that it's a different kind of trauma than mine. I understand that the immense pain that they feel is something entirely different from the pain I feel, but I wonder if they ever try to parse out my hurt. Hurt should never be a competition, but sometimes intrusive thoughts echo in my ear – they lost a son, and that is worse than losing a brother. That hurt is worse. That pain is worse. It must be so, but is my pain not significant too?

The differences between us, our hurt and trauma and grief, have made me a stranger to my parents. I no longer know if they love me for who I am, or if they feel obliged to love me because you must love family. Their love is less a whole and affectionate thing, and more a toleration of me. They tolerate that I am this way, that I have decided to leave. They tolerate that I have decided to stay away, only talking in brief spurts and never anything more. They tolerate me being family, perhaps because I am family at a distance.

If the only thing that made them love me was the connection we shared to a boy, what does that make us now that he's no longer here?

–

As a young queer, I was forbidden by my parents from speaking to my younger brothers about being not-straight. It was a joke that did it. One day, when I was home from college, my brother asked me why I didn't have a boyfriend. I replied quite plainly, as I would to anybody, 'I don't like boys.'

He burst into tears. He said that he was a boy and that meant that I must not like him.

The sensible thing, I maintain, would have been to have a conversation with him, to explain the difference between relationships between people and boyfriends or people and siblings or people and parents. We would not have needed to go into the gritty details of those differences. We could just explain that 'not liking boys' does not mean a person does not like their brothers. Instead of constructing a conversation around the different kinds of relationships people have, my parents refused to confuse my brother further, and I was barred from talking about being queer.

It was 'too complicated' a topic. But who was it complicated for? The young minds who are open to explanation or the old ones that are uncomfortable with something different? This restriction lingered with me, a hurt that I could never let go of, and a fear that I could never get over. I could not talk to my brothers about being queer and so I could not talk to them about being transgender either. They continued to use words and titles for me that hurt me. And I would continue hurting because explaining who I am was 'too complicated'.

I never brought home partners and approached the topic of attraction very neutrally or not at all. When my brothers had crushes, I thought, *How nice*, and had nothing else to say. And then I began to dress and present as even more masculine, and instead of having a conversation about it, I simply moved away. I decided that because so much of my life was related to me being queer, it would be too difficult to bring home. So I came home less and less.

I interacted with my family less and less, and I wonder now about the time I wasted not talking to my brother, not letting him know about my life. What does a ten-year-old need with my life, anyway, though? Except that when I think about his passing and the person I was when he went, I wonder what he really knew about me.

Part of me clings to the belief that there is something out there, beyond us, an afterlife. Not for any religious or spiritual reason, but only because I hope that in the spaces past living, I will get to see my brother again. Will he recognize me? Will he know who I am?

I fear that he never knew me at all. I'm afraid that he only knew an incomplete version of me, watered down so that I could make myself less complicated, less difficult for the family to explain.

Me, but not me.

—

I touched the borders of myself.

I went to feel my ends and boundaries. I went to explore the edges of my identity to see which labels felt the most like home. I wonder if all queer people do that, or if it's just us trans ones. In order to feel liberated in my identity, I needed to know which labels felt like a cage. I needed to know what would separate me from others. What made me?

Whatever dialogue I wanted to have with others, I pointed inward.

I tried on many skins, a few names, different titles. I knew 'sister' and 'daughter' felt awful, like a punch to the gut. I knew 'son' and 'brother' felt better but also felt wrong – wrong in a different direction. The neutral terms 'sibling' and 'child' felt just that, neutral. I hated 'ma'am' and 'miss' but quite liked 'boss' and even, sometimes, 'sir'. And of course, I tried James and I tried Jack, both of which felt like two different people and wholly apart from me.

I bisected and quartered myself, cut myself down, tried to find the parts that were not 'too complicated' to present to my family. What could I tell them about me that would leave as few questions as possible? What would they need to know so that I could be seen as myself and was not so inappropriate that I had to be silenced? What about me was appropriate enough to show to others?

I sifted through labels hoping that there was one that felt right. I did not find just one label and the labels I did find, the ones that I still relate to at the time of writing – the queer and trans and non-binary labels – seemed as good a home as any. When we talk about labels, we talk about them as if they are the same as stereotypes. We talk about them as if they are separate. We miss the nuance about community in identity, about partnership in labels, about friends in categories. When we talk about labels, it's as if the labels are only ever handed out. But sometimes we take them for ourselves because we find comfort in them, finally.

I tried to be anything for anybody. I tried those labels that made my insides feel as though they were becoming my outsides. I tried because I thought that was what I needed to do in order to be less complicated, that I should just accept the labels that were given to me. My inner dialogue, the only dialogue I felt allowed to have, helped me understand where I ended. Where the borders were between myself and others.

I tried, but when being anything for anybody didn't work, I knew I wanted to be just a few things. For myself, mess and all.

—

I think most people (straight people) think that being queer is only about who you do (or do not) have sex with. They think that queer as a sexuality is only about sex and, as such, is an inappropriate topic not suitable for young and sensitive ears. I can hear them asking the question, 'What does your kid brother need to know about you being queer or trans anyway?'

My experience of being queer is that it's 1 percent about sex and 99 percent about other aspects of my life. My queerness encompasses many parts of my identity, not just my sexuality. It's a part of my community and my friendships, it's a part of the media I consume, the lens through which I see the world and the perspective with which I walk through it. It tints my actions and decisions, dresses me, moves me from one place to another. Not only my queerness, but my transness as well.

So when my parents forbade me from speaking about my identity to my brothers, it wasn't just about liking or not liking boys. What they signalled to me was that they did not understand my identity, and they did not *want* to understand it. It was 'too complicated' for young minds and too different for theirs. They were not interested in the ways that my queerness coloured the other parts of my life – they were only interested in what they already assumed about being queer. Not only did they want to bar that conversation between my brothers and myself, *they* didn't want to have that conversation with my brothers. They didn't want to answer questions when I wasn't there. They were afraid of the 'inappropriateness' of my queer identity.

This is my understanding of why I have become a stranger to my family. We treat each other like acquaintances, like people who vaguely knew each other, once upon a time. We no longer go out of our way to see each other or communicate with one another. When we are in the same vicinity, we reach out only as an afterthought. I withdrew because I became 'too complicated' for them. I can only assume they ask me no questions about my life because they think they know enough. Enough to just leave me be and never ask anything more.

–

If I could turn to the last page of the relationship between myself and my parents, where would it be?

Would it have been somewhere in the 2010s? Was it there in the hospital room with my brother as he left us for some other place? Or are we still in the middle of relating to one another, still able to salvage the broken pieces of what made us a family?

I wonder, too, are our endings the same? Is the end of my relationship with them the same as the end of their relationship with me? Have I begun to think of our relationship as over while they still cling to the idea that I will return? Or do they see me as already long gone?

My brother did not know me, the full picture of me. But neither do my parents. They have not read these essays or asked me meaningful questions about my transition. And though they were there after my top surgery, in my recollection of recovery, it is my wife I remember the most, despite living with my parents at the time.

Am I the villain in this story?

I don't know.

We have never talked about this pain point in our lives, probably because we are too busy not talking about the other pain points in our lives. I hesitate to share the happy memories of my brother that appear on my phone with the large family group text, worrying that I'll upset my parents by bringing up a time when my brother was here instead of not here. I would love to talk about him as often as possible, and so many of our shared memories include him. If broaching the subject of my brother feels impossible, how else can I connect with my parents?

I wish I could turn to the last page of us now, to know whether I will be standing in an empty room by myself. I want to know if this is how it will always be, this chasm of hurt, the hollow of a boy carved in the space between us. A bridge we can never cross. I write this with hope that the last page has not already been written and that we can meet one another in the middle. Something *like* a family – just maybe not the one we were before.

–

When I settled on the labels I knew made sense for myself, when I settled on queer and trans and non-binary – the messy things that alienated me from my parents and my brothers – I sometimes wonder if I made the right choice.

Wouldn't it be easier to be binary? To be cis? To be straight?

Would life be fuller?

Would my family feel more like a family and would I have gotten back the time that I spent being a queer in New York

City? All the times I got called the f-slur on public transportation could be erased. Could I trade that time in for something else? For FaceTime with my brother? For more phone calls home? Identity crisis gone, poof. Time given back. All the worry about which friends to tell and how, just erased.

What then? Would we still be in the middle of this story, this relationship between myself and my parents?

I might not always identify the way I do right now, but that's because sometimes, as people, we grow. We evolve. We end things that don't feel right and we find new beginnings. I often end what doesn't feel right. I no longer have the time or the patience to try to make those uncomfortable things feel comfortable.

After my brother, one of those uncomfortable things that I could no longer make comfortable was trying to be a watered-down version of myself in front of my family. So much of my life is about, and revolves around, being queer. Everything from my friends to my relationship with my wife. I even bring my queerness with me to work. I go to gay bars; I consume queer and trans media; I read LGBTQ+ stories and prioritize authors from marginalized communities. So much of the very happy, fulfilled life I now live is made up of queerness.

And yet, there is this page that I keep thinking about, that I long to turn to, just to know. Has it happened? Is it over? Am I lost in a crowd or standing in an empty room?

Will my parents ever want to know about my queer and trans life? I have tried to imagine a path that would let me open myself up to them, to make *their* uncomfortable more comfortable, but the path has always been blocked by past hurt that I cannot move aside.

—

All things end. My brother ended. Each of these essays has an end. This book, soon, will end. Relationships end, like the ones between myself and my family. Each of us.

But things begin anew, too. Some things are just pauses, brief moments between sequels. I think that can happen with people. Sometimes we take long stretches away from one another, become strangers to parse out our hurt and to find ourselves. And then we can come back and meet as different people, and maybe those different people will be compatible once more.

Maybe that compatibility is like family, again.

That way things don't have to be so final, don't have to end so sadly, with each of us alone. Because some ends aren't just standing in empty rooms or walking away from a scene. Some ends are the clatter of dinnerware and noise, records playing softly. Some ends are laughs, caught by the wind, lilting to eternity. Some ends are happy and full, after so much hurt and grief.

I hope that for us. A happy end, all of us together. A neat and final flip of the page.

Acknowledgements

These essays would not exist without the community that holds me up each and every day, who make this life so worth living.

Thank you to my wonderful friends around the world, from the bottom of my deep, dark heart. In no particular order, deep thanks to Arielle Duhaime-Ross and Meredith Cornelius (and Reggie too, though she is of no help with this particular writing). To Amy Kuhn and Erin Hogeboom and Juneau, who I love so dearly. To the Spacones, each and every one of you – Laurie and Chris and Mitch and Jenny. To my wife's wife Liz Spacone, who was the sole witness to our wedding during the pandemic. To Amanda Krueger, for singing Adele with me on the 101. To Kaitlyn Rich and Austin Bening, Maple's stewards. To Annalise Domenighini, Paula Ersly, and Dr Kylie Langlois, soup sluts forever. To E. J. Judge and Dax Dupuy. To Celina Enriquez, Caroline Bargo, Katherine Rocha and Dalia Guerrera.

To the novice lads of the UCD Boat Club from 2018 to 2019. To the creative writing MA cohort of the same year and to our instructors.

To Skein Press! Fionnuala and Gráinne, who provided wonderful insight that made me make sense, and Nidhi, who not only believed in the work that I was writing but who also listened to me clack away on that godawful keyboard and play 'On the Nature of Daylight' on repeat (I still play the song repeatedly but I did upgrade my keyboard).

To Max Richter for *The Blue Notebooks (15 Years)*, Charli XCX for *Charli* and *Number 1 Angel*, and Joe Hisaishi.

To Sinéad Gleeson and Julie Morrissey.

To fan fiction.

To trans and non-binary folk who came before me and to trans and non-binary folk who come after me.

To Lyon-Martin Health Services, to Apicha Community Health Center, to UCSF. To Felice de la Cerna and Dr Esther Kim.

Thank you to my family and all our heavy hearts and all the butterflies and crows that get sent to us. Who will we be, under the sea?

Thank you to my family and all our light hearts, for 'I'm just sayin'' and 'Everything will work out.' Indeed it does.

And thank you to Emily, my love. I hope to love you until the sun burns out. I hope you'll love me until at least then too.